RECESS

From Dodgeball to Double Dutch:
Classic Games for Players of Today

Ben Applebaum and Dan DiSorbo
with Michael Ferrari

Insights from Julia Askin, Nick Benas, Ben Blatt, Sean Effel,
Steve Frasher, Julian Gluck, Mike Judd, Sam Kass, Duncan Little,
David Lowry, Ed Prentiss, Alex Smith, and Chris Spatola

CHRONICLE BOOKS
SAN FRANCISCO

Attention Players, Parents, and Recess Fans Around the World

The games described in this book can be dangerous—and we're talking more than scraped knees and bruised egos. Injuries, sometimes even serious ones, can happen. Please participate in these activities with caution and under the supervision of adults. The authors and publishers expressly disclaim liability from any injury, damage, or distress that result from engaging in any of the activities described in this book.

Library of Congress Cataloging-in-Publication Data available.

ISBN: 978-1-4521-3850-3

Manufactured in China

Designed by MacFadden & Thorpe

Funnel Ball is a registered trademark of BCI Burke Company, LLC.
Louisville Slugger is a registered trademark of Wilson Sporting Goods Co.
National Dodgeball League is a registered trademark of National
  Dodgeball League, Inc.
Spalding and Spaldeen are registered trademarks of Russell Brand, LLC.
WAKA is a registered trademark of WAKA Kickball & Social Sports.
Wiffle is a registered trademark of The Wiffle Ball, Inc.

10 9 8 7 6 5 4 3 2 1

Chronicle Books LLC
680 Second Street
San Francisco, California 94107
www.chroniclebooks.com

Contents of Fun

Introduction

"The true object of all human life is play."
— **Gilbert K. Chesterton**

In a world with more play buttons than playgrounds, more handhelds than handballs, fewer people are taking full advantage of their spare time. They're opting to zone out rather than getting out.

But we say it's time to make a change. It's time to turn downtime into playtime. It's time to turn off the screens, pump up the balls, and actually play together. And ultimately, it's time to forget about growing up, and remember how to play like kids again.

That's why we are here to celebrate recess, not just the break in the day, but also the whole state of mind. We want you to rediscover your favorite games and to explore new ones, to be inspired by tradition, and to use your creativity to create competitions of your very own. But above all, we want you to share and enjoy these games with someone—a child, a classmate, a coworker, a new friend.

We have compiled all the greatest recess games into the one timeless device suitable for such an ageless and prestigious activity—a book.

But we don't want you just to read this book; we want you to play it. We want you to pick up a rope and skip it, to find a marble and shoot it, to gather your friends together, young and old, for some friendly competition.

Of course, there is no one way to play any one game. Nearly all of these games existed well before the Internet, some of them even before the printing press. So it's no surprise that there are hundreds, if not thousands, of playing variations as different groups passed down their rules from kid to kid, neighborhood to neighborhood, generation to generation.

We've worked to hone each entry for the optimal game play; presenting every game in its most popular form with straight-forward rules and regulations, and tips on how to maximize fun and inclusion. We've also included various additional rules and alternate versions alongside the basic rules of play to allow you to put your own spin on it. Think of it as a recess remix kit, giving you the tools to take a great game and make it your own.

With all this in mind, we invite you to join us in helping bring back all the joys of recess for everyone.

Game on, everyone.
Game on.

HOMEROOM
RECESS
BASICS

Ring the bell, Recess is about to begin

Just play. Have fun. Enjoy the game.
— Michael Jordan

Playing around is too important to play around with. Knowing just how recess works, what rules to follow, how to master each game's unique skills, and how you can make the most of it are all just as important as knowing which game you're going to choose and who you want to have on your team.

While there's something to be said about throwing the rules to the wind and seeing what happens, success always favors a prepared mind—and a willing body. This first section will cover the basics: from picking Firsts to victory celebrations and everything in between.

How to Recess

Before you jump right in, it's time to get good at having a good time. So we've created an easy-to-remember Ode to Recess as a simple acronym (R-E-C-E-S-S) to help you understand the basics of what it takes to be a champion of any playing field.

R = RESPECT

The first step to fun is respecting all the rules of the games and respecting all the players involved—never picking on anyone, never leaving anyone out, and especially never bullying anyone.

E = EFFORT

You don't have to be the best, but you should always try your best. Giving your full effort is all it takes to harness the full fun potential of any game, for yourself and your teammates.

C = COMPETITION

There's nothing wrong with playful competition. Play to win, but don't be a sore loser or a bad winner. It's never too early to practice sportsmanship and begin fostering a healthy competitive spirit.

E = EXERCISE

Recess games give you plenty of good exercise without having to think about "exercise." Get out there, get healthy, and don't worry—bumps and bruises are badges to be worn with pride!

S = SOCIAL

Aside from teamwork, play allows for other great social experiences that can improve confidence, build relationships, and grow friendships.

S = SAFETY

This comes last in our list, but should be the first thing you think about when playing. It's never fun to get hurt, and it's never cool to hurt others. Always follow the rules and never do anything that could hurt yourself or others.

WORLD OF PLAY

In Australia, a morning recess is often called "little lunch" to differentiate it from the real "big lunch" break at midday.

The Value of Recess for Kids

A lot of people assume that recess is all about running around and playing games, and they're right! What they don't realize is that running and playing are vital functions to the developmental process. Here are just some of the benefits of recess:

A Cognitive Kick in the Pants

Research has shown that kids who participate in recess and playful activities are not only less fidgety and more focused, but they also have higher test scores and a better attitude toward school. In fact, studies have proven that this break in the day gives the brain enough time to relax and prepare for the next lesson.

A Course in Society 101

The recess yard almost perfectly simulates normal society and gives children valuable training in decision making, cooperation, and leadership. Additionally, the social inter-action allowed by recess stimulates the mind and can help students better learn and retain information.

Couch Potato Prevention

Studies show that children who had recess before lunch made better decisions about their food choices afterward. Even more important, research has shown that kids who remain sedentary during the school day remain sedentary when they get home. This means that breaking the school day apart with physical activity has a lasting effect on children's home lives.

The Value of Recess for Grown-Ups

You're only young once, but you can play games your entire life . . . and you should, according to experts like psychiatrist Stuart Brown, MD. In his book *Play*, Brown compares play to oxygen, writing, ". . . it's all around us, yet goes mostly unnoticed or unappreciated until it is missing."

Brown isn't the only one who feels that way, either. Experts of all flavors have come to the same conclusion: If you want to live a happy life, you have to play hard for it. As follows are some of the other benefits grownups can reap from recess:

Snuff Out Stress
Play is one of the easiest ways to relieve stress, thanks to endorphins, the body's natural feel-good chemicals. Endorphins are released during play to create an overall sense of good vibes in your mind and throughout your body, making it one of the easiest ways to combat stress, which has been shown to cause 75 to 90 percent of all doctors' visits.

Boost Your Brain
Playing around offers plenty of challenges—such as figuring out how to dominate in Tic Tac Toe or the best way to bean your buddy with a dodgeball. These challenges exercise the brain and give it a chance to flex its squishy muscles. All this helps the brain function better, think quicker, and retain memories more easily.

Bond with Buddies

Socializing over a game is not only good for laughs, it's also good for emotional development. Sharing and laughing with others helps foster compassion, trust, and empathy, which in turn help improve relationships both on and off the playground.

Keeps You Kicking Longer

A wise man once said you're only as young as you feel, and play has been one of the few things that guarantees you'll feel younger for longer. Adults who regularly make time for play typically have more energy and improved health compared to those who don't, making play a vital ingredient in staying healthy for your entire life.[4]

The Difference Between Competition and Bullying

Fun and games are all fun and games, until they're not, like when competition turns overly aggressive and harmful. That's not to say you should stay away from competition altogether—as research points out, competition can be a powerful tool in moderation. It's when it gets extreme that it floats into dangerous bullying waters.

Competition and bullying are two very different things with very different outcomes. Use the following quick breakdown to help keep you more of a player than a hater.

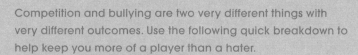

A COMPETITIVE PLAYER	A BULLYING PLAYER
Engages in horseplay, smack talk, and the occasional wisecrack	Engages in violence, insults, and mean-spirited tactics
Makes it all about the game	Makes it personal and hurtful
Keeps the competition all about the other team	Keeps singling out individuals to target
Brings out the best in his teammates and opponents	Brings out the worst in other players
Leaves the winner feeling victorious and the loser feeling humbled	Leaves the winner feeling superior and the loser feeling ashamed
Empowers other players and gives them a reason for a rematch	Belittles players and makes them want to leave the playing field

RULES OF PLAY

While recess may be all about free play, it's not a free-for-all. While every game has its rules—see pages 22 through 237—there are those universal rules of the playground that we can all be reminded of.

- **NO CRYING OR MAKING OTHERS CRY**
  Recess is all about fun, and crying has no part in that. So unless you're getting teary over a triumphant win, keep your eyes dry.

- **NO TATTLING**
  Life's not fair, and neither is being forced out because someone got you with a cheap shot. Still, that's no reason to tell on someone. Tattling puts the whole game at risk, so if you have a problem, figure it out player to player or keep it to yourself and refocus your energy on the game.

- **NO CHEATING**
  Nobody likes a cheater, nobody. Not even cheaters like cheaters. So play fair or don't play at all.

- **ONCE YOU QUIT, YOU'RE OUT**
  Nobody likes a quitter either—not only is it cowardly, but it messes up the teams. Because of that, anyone who quits during a game is not allowed back on the team until the start of a new game, and that's only if other players allow it.

- **GAMES ARE PICKED BY MAJORITY RULES**
  The game that has the most people voting to play it is the game that gets played. If you don't like it, find another group.

- **NO HEAD SHOTS**
  Though sometimes funny to watch, hitting someone in the head with a ball is very painful and can be extremely dangerous. Nobody wants to spend recess at the school nurse, so keep all shots below the neck.

- **NO CROTCH SHOTS**
  Being hit in a sensitive area is a sensitive subject. So we'll just leave it at this: no going for the groin.

- **NO MAKING UP YOUR OWN RULES**
  Each game has rules. If you don't know them, ask before you begin to play and don't go trying to make yours up once everyone starts playing (unless it's part of the game). If you think a rule is dumb or unfair, take it up with the rest of the players before starting the game and change it together.

- **NO RUNNING OFF WITH BALLS OR EQUIPMENT**
  Once a game starts, the equipment belongs to the teams using it. Nobody else is allowed to run off with it for their own game until the original teams are done with it.

- **NO OVERUSE OF TIME-OUT**
  Calling time-out comes with great responsibility.

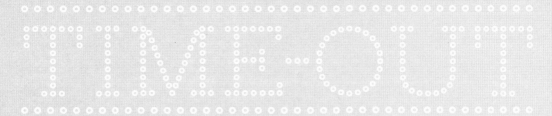

TIMEOUT

The Ins and Outs of Time-Outs

Time-outs give everyone a chance to stop for a second and figure out what's going on. But while time-outs are an important part of game play, proper use and control needs to be practiced to prevent time-outs from happening too often.

ACCEPTABLE REASONS FOR CALLING TIME-OUT	UNACCEPTABLE REASONS FOR CALLING TIME-OUT
Equipment gets lost or broken	Someone gets bored
Someone *needs* to go to the bathroom	Someone *wants* to go to the bathroom
Confusion about the rules	Someone gets frustrated about losing
Someone gets seriously hurt	Someone gets nonseriously hurt (only a *boo-boo*)

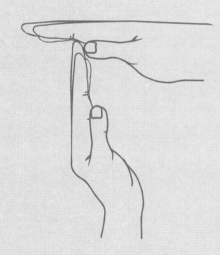

How to Properly Call Time-Out

There are a number of different ways that a player can call time-out.

The Hand "T"
A classic used by the pros, this move involves making your hands flat and intersecting them so they look like a "T." Not only does this catch people's attention, but it looks cool, too!

Hand Raise
While some may argue that raising your hand should be saved for the classroom, this easy method will quickly get noticed by other players.

Yell "Time"
Loud, proud, and forceful, simply yelling "Time" will freeze everyone in their track and capture their attention.

DECIDING FIRSTS

The only thing more important than knowing the rules to a game is knowing who is up first, or as it's simply known, Firsts. Arguments over who has Firsts have been around almost as long as recess itself. Following is a list of some of the most common solutions to this problem:

Coin Flip

One of the simplest decision devices if you have a coin handy, is to just flip it and call it in the air. Whoever guesses right gets Firsts. The only tricky part is deciding how to land the coin.

1 Letting it fall is the preferred method for sporting events the world over. It may deliver a more neutral result since it has no human element to it, but it could cause the coin to bounce around and get lost.

2 In the palm and flip is another version—the coin is caught in an open palm and then immediately flipped over onto the back of the catcher's hand. This takes some hand-eye coordination and the coin could be dropped. Resulting, of course, in the first option.

Whichever option you choose, make sure everyone agrees that the call is final!

Coach Says . . .

While a lot of people think winning a coin toss is all up to chance, there is a way to increase your odds of winning. The secret is to call "tails" every time. The reason is simple: the heads side of the coin weighs just a little more than the tails side, so the coin lands "face down" slightly more often.

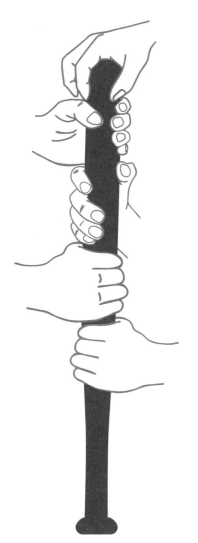

Dibs

Dibs is a classic kickoff for any bat and ball game. A representative from one team grabs the fat end of the bat. The other team's rep grabs the bat with his hand—placing it above his opponent's hand. Players alternate in this pattern moving upward—hand on top of hand. The last one to grab the top of the bat without going over the top gets Firsts.

Coach Says . . .

Done with dibs? Not so fast—don't forget the Kick Rule! If the final person grabs the knob at the top with his fingertips, the opponent has one chance to kick the bat. If the bat is knocked out of his hand, the kicker wins Firsts. If it stays put, the person holding the bat wins Firsts.

Drawing Straws

A classic that comes from more rural areas, drawing straws has long been used to single out the lucky person who gets Firsts. Originally, straws of hay were used for this, but you can use anything similar for this task—straws from a broom, drinking straws, and blades of grass all work well. Select enough straws so there is one for each person playing. Cut or tear each straw to make sure they are all different lengths. Then, one person takes all of them, mixes them up and presents them to the players through a closed hand with the straws sticking out so it's impossible to know which is longest. Each player picks one straw, and the person with the longest straw gets Firsts.

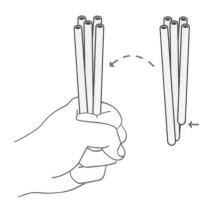

Rock-Paper-Scissors

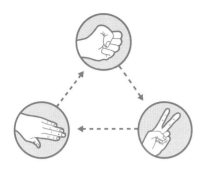

The classic battle of wits and hands, Rock-Paper-Scissors is almost intense enough to be a recess game itself. Some have traced its history to an old Chinese game called Hand Control from 200 B.C. Today, it's used by judges, auctioneers, and of course, players of every sort of game.

The game play is simple. Two players stand across from each other with clenched fists extended. They move their fists in vertical pounding motion to a count of three (or to the name "Rock, Paper, Scissors" or "Ro, Sham, Bo"). On the fourth beat, they say either "go" or "throw" and simultaneously reveal one of three symbols. On most recess yards, Rock-Paper-Scissors goes by the best of three rules with no redoes.

ROCK-PAPER-SCISSORS DECODED

WARNING: You are about to read the golden key that will unlock dominance in Rock-Paper-Scissors. We recommend you black out this section with a marker before sharing the book with your friends. Your success will last as long as they don't read this.

1. Most competitive players will favor the most aggressive choice "rock."[5]

2. According a study of over 350 subjects, if people win, they are more likely to stick with the same sign.[6]

3. But when people lose, they don't switch willy-nilly. They are likely to rotate in a clockwise direction, from rock to paper to scissors.

What you do with this theory is up to you. If you keep your opponent from overthinking their choices, you can beat an opponent in a "best of three" with "Paper" then "Scissors." Now prepare to win those Firsts.

Rock-Paper-Scissors-Spock-Lizard

Rock-Paper-Scissors-Spock-Lizard was created by software developer Sam Kass to eliminate the common problem with Rock-Paper-Scissors: the game ending in a tie. With the addition of two new gestures—the Lizard and Spock's Vulcan salute from Star Trek—the probability of a tie is greatly reduced as the complexity of the game is increased. Here's how it works.

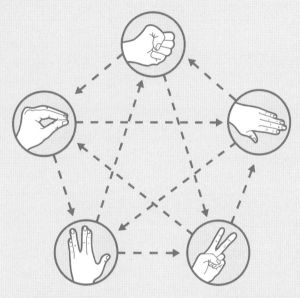

- Rock crushes Lizard
- Rock crushes Scissors
- Paper disproves Spock
- Paper covers Rock
- Scissors decapitates Lizard
- Scissors cuts Paper
- Spock vaporizes Rock
- Spock bends Scissors
- Lizard poisons Spock

It's worth noting that some people struggle with making the Spock sign, so Scissors or Rock can have an advantage. On the other hand (literally) Lizard has an advantage according to Sam Kass since "it's fun to pretend to eat other people's hands if you win."

ADDITIONAL FIRST TECHNIQUES

Pick a Number

One player thinks of a number between one and five. She holds that number of fingers out behind her back. If another player can guess it, they get Firsts.

Two-Hand Monty

With a pebble in hand, one player shuffles the pebble or any small object from hand to hand behind his back. When he's done, he presents both hands to the other player. If the player can correctly guess which hand the pebble is in, she gets Firsts.

Odd Even

One player calls "odds" and the other calls "evens." On the count of three, each player either sticks out one finger or two fingers. If the total amount of fingers showing on both hands adds up to two or four, then the player who called "evens" wins; if the total of all fingers adds up to three, then the player who called "odds" wins. It sounds like a lot of math, but it's actually really simple.

PICKING TEAMS

Some games require teams. And every great team on the recess yard is more than the sum of its parts. In other words, it takes more than great players to make a team. Building a solid team takes chemistry, camaraderie, and a little bit of luck to properly pull it off.

The Captain Method is the most common process. Everyone nominates two people to be team captains, and lead their respective teams. Once captains are picked and Firsts are decided, it's time to assemble. While the easy tactic would just be to pick the best players, that's not always possible to determine and it doesn't always make for the best game. Here are some tips and considerations for picking the best possible team:

Balance is Key

The best teams are the ones that are well rounded. Try to keep your team diverse and stacked with players of different heights, weights, ages, and skill levels. For instance, you don't want a dodgeball team full of only great throwers; you want a team that has great throwers, great catchers, and nimble dodgers.

Team Chemistry

We're not talking about science class, here. This chemistry refers to how well players get along with each other. For instance picking two best friends to be on the same team could be much more valuable than having two superstar players since best friends already have a strong bond.

Don't Underestimate the Underdog

Sometimes hard work is more valuable than skill, and underdogs always try harder since nobody thinks they can win. Put a few on your team and use their drive to your advantage.

ADDITIONAL TEAM PICKING TECHNIQUES

Eenie Meenie

This is one of a number of counting-out rhymes that help randomly select (or deselect) potential players. To use it, gather everyone around in a circle, with one player reciting, "Eenie, meenie, miney, moe, catch a tiger by the toe, if he hollers, let him go. Eenie, meenie, miney, moe," while pointing at the next player in the circle as you say each word. The person you're pointing at as you say "moe" at the end of the rhyme gets Firsts.

Coach Says . . .

If you want to avoid getting picked last, remember to choose games you're good at, show the captain you're ready with your best game face, or, if all else fails, just jump and yell, "Oh oh oh, pick me, pick me!"

Ip Dip Doo

The first player says, "Ip Dip Doo" and points to another player who must then say, "Ip Dip Doo," plus add a rhyming phrase to it. He points at a third player who must say, "Ip Dip Doo," repeat the second rhyming phrase, and then add a new rhyming phrase, and so on. When a player messes up, he's out of the running. Last person remaining gets Firsts!

One Potato, Two Potato

Everyone stands in a circle and sticks in two fists. They all chant, "One potato, two potato, three potato, four! Five potato, six potato, seven potato, more!" While chanting, one player goes around the inside of the circle and bops her fist on each player's fist when each number is said. The first player who gets bopped on the word "more" is out. This is repeated until there's only one fist left, and the owner of said fist gets Firsts.

Other Types of Teams

While the Team Captain Method is the most popular way to pick teams, it's only one of many ways to pick sides.

Boys vs. Girls

A good, old-fashioned battle of the sexes is still one of the best ways to kick things off.

Neighborhood vs. Neighborhood, Classroom vs. Classroom, or Grade vs. Grade

The point is, you're all already part of teams, so use that setup to your advantage.

The Count Off

This is a democratic solution if there ever was one. All players line up and call out numbers in order until everyone has a number. Odds are on one team, evens on the other.

Same Teams As Last Time

Since you spent so much time coming up with teams the last time you played, why not just stick with it?

Official Recess Team Name Generator

When recess is just a few precious minutes long, you can't afford to spend that time arguing about the best name for your team. That's where this list comes in handy. We've developed this state-of-the-art name generator. Simply choose one word from each column and you will have a fresh, 100-percent guaranteed awesome team name.

Fighting	Spider Monkeys
Flying	Brawlers
Insane	Liquidators
Cross-Eyed	Ballers
Backward	Spikers
Spike-Fisted	Marauders
Red Rubber	Spaldeens
Mutha-Luvin'	Grounders
Blacktop	Lunch Ladies
Rainy Day	Dawgs
Four-Squarin'	Warriors
Fierce	Monitors
Backhanded	Rats
Gym Class	Teachers
Rockin-Rolling	Mercy Killers
Nasty	Kickers
30-Minute	Palmers
Street Corner	Blasters
Chalky	Crawlers
Dodgy	Dodgers

An Ode to Playground Equipment

The literal landscape of the playground has changed from generation to generation. Occasionally, equipment that was once considered harmless fun becomes a public enemy. And when that happens, they disappear. But some remain—and are definitely worth celebrating.

MERRY-GO-ROUND

Don't be fooled by visions of a relaxing spin on a carousel. The real fun is trying to hold on as your so-called friends spin the platform at an increasingly nausea-inducing speed. Whoever can avoid being tossed off—or tossing cookies—wins.

TIRE SWING

Some of the newer plastic playgrounds have replica tire swings, but we're talking about the real deal. On paper there seems no way a giant truck tire, heavy gauge metal chains, and industrial fasteners should ever be around children. But one session of mind-bending, stomach twisting twirls and you'll put this in the hall of fame.

SPRINGY ANIMAL THINGS

Sure they look unassuming, but these are miniature thrill rides. Enough rocking back and forth and you might just get flung out of your seat.

FUNNEL BALL

For a few years in the 1970s and 80s, Funnel Ball made a run at becoming something of a standard on the recess yard. It involves throwing a rubber ball up into a bucket to score points. The amount of points awarded for each shot is not determined by where a player shoots but by the very random whims of the funnel. It's a classic!

GIANT STRIDE

Also known as the Octopus or the Big Strike, this is a feat of fun engineering. The spinning handles allow you to run and take giant strides around the pole. Get enough speed and you can take off—literally.

FAST METAL SLIDES

Take a piece of metal, put it at a dangerously steep angle, and heat it for at least six hours in the scalding sun. Congratulations, you've just created one of the most treacherous and most exciting pieces of equipment in all of the playground land.

1 FIRST PERIOD
HAND GAMES

The Original Handheld Games

It is better to play than do nothing.
— Confucius

It's time to look past electronic handheld technology and get "digital" in the more traditional way—with the finger digits of the human hand. There are a lot of entertaining and engaging games that are always literally within reach. But don't let the fact that these games don't involve fancy equipment or a large field fool you into thinking they're boring. These hand games are full of slapping, clapping, soulful singing, and the occasional punch.

HAND SLAPS
Two People, Four Hands, No Holds Barred

Game Stats

STYLE: Reaction game
PLAYERS: Two
REQUIREMENTS:
Four hands
SKILLS:
Hand-eye coordination
Pain tolerance
Patience

- - - - - - - - - -

ALSO KNOWN AS

Hot hands
Red Hands
Red Tomato
Slap Jack
Slap Tennis
Slaps
Slapsies
Wiggle Waggle

WHAT IT IS

This simple hand competition is gaming at its best. It tests players' hand-eye speed, fake-out ability, and pain threshold. What makes it so great and so popular is that it requires no space, makes little noise (other than slapping and the occasional whimper), lacks complicated rules, and is utterly equipment-free. Most impressive, however, is that it includes something rare in today's world: safe danger. The threat of a stinging slap to the hand is enough to trigger adrenaline without causing much damage.

WHAT'S THE POINT?

The most common game play is to continue to stay in the dominant position as long as possible; in other words, you want to spend more time being the slapper than the slappee. The additional goal of the game is to get your opponent to throw in the towel due to increasing levels of either pain or frustration. Some versions involve earning points, but we prefer to the open-ended version that deals in the economy of slaps.

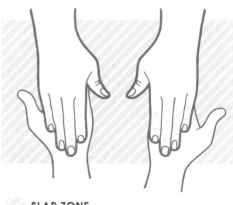

SLAP ZONE

HOW YOU PLAY

① Assume the position After Firsts are decided, the players stand face-to-face about two feet apart with hands outstretched a little above waist height. Player one (the slapper) places her hands palms up and shoulder-width apart. Player two (the slappee) signals the start of play when she places her hands palm down—directly over and lightly touching player one's upturned hands.

② Slapping on offense
The slapper is on offense and attempts to bring her hands over to slap the tops of the slappee's hands. The slapper can strike one hand or both hands at the same time. A slap is clean when contact is made on any part of the slappee's hands within the slap zone (see illustration). As long as the slap connects, the slapper remains on offense.

③ Dodging on Defense
The slappee's job is simple: avoid the slap. She must elude the hit by moving her hands outside the slap zone before the slapper can make contact. If the slapper misses, then the roles are flipped—the slapper becomes the slappee and the power dynamics are reversed.

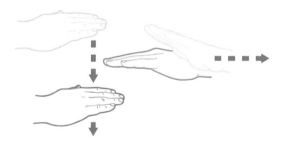

Coach Says . . .

Some people recommend that the hands hover a half-inch apart, but we prefer the closer hand-to-hand combat position.

4 Issuing penalty slaps

Penalty slapping polices the players and keeps the game play true. To issue these penalties, the game is paused and the receiver must take the slap without dodging. There are two scenarios for which this can occur:

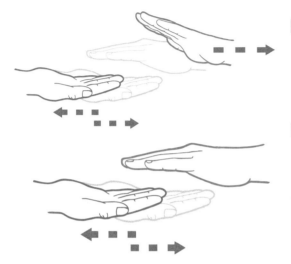

A a slappee is hit with a penalty slap when she commits three flinches. A flinch is when a player preemptively moves their hands in a dodge motion despite the slapper not making a slap movement;

B a slapper is hit with a penalty *and* must reverse to the slappee position when they make contact with the slappee's hand outside of the slap zone, above the slappee's wrist, or they commit a balk. A balk is when the slapper tries to bait the slappee into flinching but makes a partial slap motion and never follows through.

5 The Pain of Defeat

This back and forth continues until one player taps out due to pain, or until recess is over.

SLAPPING TECHNIQUES

The Double Slap

This is when the slapper hits both of the slappee's hands at the same time.

The Crossover

This is a powerful, though risky, slap that involves the slapper going across and connecting with the opposite hand of the slappee. For example, the slapper uses her right hand to smack the right hand of her opponent.

The Two-on-One Slap

A rare move that requires the slapper to use both hands to connect with one of the slappee's hands. While this doesn't hurt twice as much, it does provide a blow to the slappee's self-esteem.

The Tag

This is a slap that counts as a hit, but doesn't deliver any pain. Often, it's only the slapper's fingers that connect with the top of the slappee's hand.

The Stinger

This is the opposite of the tag: it's a fully painful smack that includes maximum skin-to-skin contact that hits with a loud slap and results in a lasting sting.

EXPERT STRATEGIES

The Classic Misdirect

Like a magician working the crowd, the slapper can maintain control by directing the slappee's attention away from the intended strike. The easiest form of misdirection is when the slapper uses her eyes to fixate on one hand, luring the slappee's attention toward it before hitting the other hand.

The Distracted Destroyer

This approach is similar to Muhammad Ali's rope-a-dope strategy: lull your opponent into thinking you're too preoccupied and unfocused to be a serious competitor. Once they become distracted by your distracted behavior, you unleash a surprise attack of slaps.

The Slap Storm

While this game is known for requiring very little exertion, a rapid succession of slaps from each side at a blistering pace is a powerful strategy to put your opponent on their heels— and their hands eventually on ice. Only a short burst of this slap storm is needed to throw them off their game for rounds to come.

The Slow Simmer

Although many consider this a game of the hands, it's ultimately a game of the mind. A proven strategy is to allow the nerves and jumpiness of your opponent to work in your favor. On offense, just let the clock tick. The longer you wait between slaps, the more likely your opponent will flinch, allowing you to administer penalty slaps.

SAFETY PATROL: Slapping should hurt, not harm. To avoid serious injury, all rings and bracelets should be removed before playing. And while some redness in the hands is expected, play should be stopped if there are any welts, cuts, or bruises, that is, to body parts rather than egos.

WORLD OF PLAY

FUN FACT

There is no clear explanation why a wet slap creates more impact than a dry slap. One theory is that wet skin is suppler and makes more surface area to create a belly-flop effect. Another theory is that it's louder and just assumed to be more painful. The only way to find out is to keep experimenting.

The Numb Waiter

The double pun in the title is doubly intended. This controversial, sacrificial strategy involves allowing one's hand to actually receive many slaps early in the game to induce a numbing sensation. It is believed that this can inoculate the hand from future stingers.

OPTIONAL RULES
Eye Contact

Players must maintain eye contact during the whole game—trusting only on peripheral vision and their sixth sense.

No Crossovers

Possibly due to the potential pain generated from classic crossover slaps, some players ban that slap from the game play.

Two-Touch Minimum

This rule states that the slapper must always use a double slap technique and connect with both hands.

Lick Penalty Slap

The administrator of the penalty slap licks the tops of their own fingers on the striking hand. With the other hand, they hold the slappee's forearm—wrist side up. The slap is delivered just above the wrist and the combination of the soft forearm skin and wet, fingers creates an intense sting.

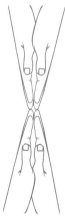

OTHER WAYS TO PLAY
Double Prayer

This version of the game is perfect for tighter quarters. The slapper and slappee start off by facing each other with hands in identical prayer-like positions with middle fingertips touching. The slapper uses single-handed strikes on either side of the slappee's hands. On defense, the slappee moves her hands up and down to dodge the strikes—making sure to keep them together at all times.

Quick Draw

Like the double prayer formation, the slappee places her hands together out in front, but the slapper starts from a position with her hands at her hips—like an Old West gunslinger. The game play continues as normal.

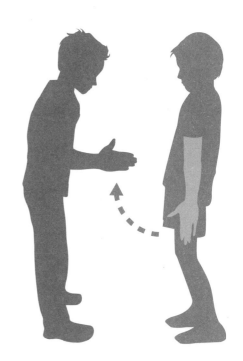

Chinese Hot Hands

This slugfest is not for the squeamish or anyone with carpal tunnel syndrome. Players face each other and interlock their left hands at their fingers. Now, the slapping begins. Each player takes a turn whacking the top of their opponent's left hand with their right one. This volley continues until one player can no longer stand the pain and breaks his grip, thus surrendering.

THUMB WRESTLING
One, Two, Three, Four, We Declare a Classic

Game Stats

STYLE: Close combat game

PLAYERS: Two

REQUIREMENTS:
Two thumbs

SKILLS:
Hand-eye coordination
Grip strength
Thumb agility

- - - - - - - - - -

ALSO KNOWN AS
Thumb Wars
Thumb-a-War
Thumb Battles

WHAT IT IS
Thumb Wrestling is a legendary gladiator battle brought down to smaller, stubbier proportions. It brings all of the excitement of professional wrestling, all the classism of Greco-Roman, all the physicality of Mixed Martial Arts (MMA) into a portable (and less painful) form. While the physical element is undeniable, the beauty of this game is that sheer force is not the point. To emerge victorious, one must have a full suite of skills—strength, speed, flexibility, and intelligence—packed into his thumbs.

WHAT'S THE POINT?
The point is to pin. As with all wrestling, a "pin" is a way to demonstrate complete control and mastery over one's opponent. A pin in Thumb Wrestling is when an opponent's thumb is rendered immobile for a predetermined period of time. Because matches can often be quite quick, this game is usually played as a best-of-five series.

HOW YOU PLAY
1 Get a grip
The grip is the foundation of the game. A great grip establishes the starting position for the action ahead.

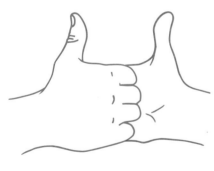

First, the fingers should be tightly interlocked. A firm grip is encouraged—digging your fingernails into your opponent's flesh, however, is not. Secondly, if the game is played standing up, the hands must be level both horizontally and vertically. If, however, it is played on a table, the forearms should be on the tabletop to ensure a level playing field. At all times, the unused hand must remain behind the back.

Finally, the thumbs of each player should be ramrod straight. Not only does this demonstrate that each player is ready to compete, it demonstrates a respect for the game's tradition.

❷ Chant the chant

It's important to kick off the match in a way that allows both competitors to start at the same time (and alert everyone within earshot that a match has commenced). While there are some small variations, the Thumb War Chant and side-to-side motion is nearly universal and an important part of the tradition.

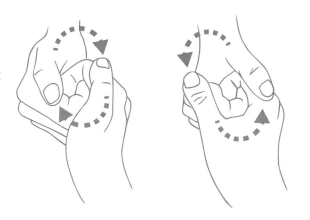

One, two, three, four,
I declare a Thumb War.

❸ Mix it up

Go for it. A good match puts the opposable in opposable thumbs.

❹ Avoid fouls

In a best of five series, a violation of one of the rules should result in the equivalent of the pin. The major fouls include: **(a)** breaking the grip and pulling your hand away, **(b)** twisting an opponent's arm or wrist for an advantage **(c)** using a finger to interfere with the match, and **(d)** jerking of the opponent's hand to catch them off guard.

SAFETY PATROL: This is thumb wrestling, not thumb scratching. Thumbnails need to be kept short and can never, we repeat never, be used offensively.

❺ Pin to win

In full-body wrestling, a three-count is enough to decide a winner. But in this game, it is required that the pin is held for a longer period. While some traditions suggest a ten-count, we side with the governing body of the World Thumb Wrestling Championship and recommend that a pin must be held for the length of time it takes to say:

One, two, three, four,
I win a Thumb War!

PINNING TECHNIQUES

Nail Pin

This is the most common but least secure pinning technique. The pinner holds down the opponent's thumb by applying pressure to the top of the thumbnail. Since it's a forward-facing flat surface, it's easy to try to pin them this way, but it's also easy for them to slip out and escape.

First Knuckle Pin

This is a much more professional approach. The pinner applies pressure directly to the opponent's first knuckle, along with the thumbnail. While this is more secure than the nail pin, the opponent still has enough room to wriggle free.

Second Knuckle Pin

This is the thumb equivalent of a headlock. It does take more strength to apply, but done right, it can immobilize the opponent's thumb and, quite possibly, their willpower.

EXPERT STRATEGIES

The Lightning Strike

This is an immediate and aggressive attack coming right off the chant. In most cases, a counterclockwise move will provide the most power and reach. It will catch them off guard and bring the noise.

The Rope-a-Dope

Sometimes you need to let your opponents beat themselves. Allow your opponent to come out swinging while you hang back, letting them make strikes against your thumb base while keeping your thumb tip out reach. Wait for them to extend their thumb too far and attack their exposed position.

The Tip Flip

If you are feeling even more adventurous, you can attempt to make a risky self-sacrifice and offer up your thumbnail for an ostensibly easy pin. When they take the bait, dramatically feign disappointment. As soon as they think victory is within sight, slip out of their light hold to catch them off guard for a counter attack.

OPTIONAL RULES

Alternate chants—there are several other popular chants to kick off the match. Familiarize yourself with all of them so that you're always ready when it's time to rumble.

A
> *One, two, three, four,*
> *I declare a Thumb War.*
> *Five, six, seven, eight,*
> *Try to keep your thumb straight.*

C
> *One, two, three, four,*
> *I declare a Thumb War.*
> *Four, three, two, one,*
> *Who will be the strongest thumb?*

B
> *One, two, three, four,*
> *I declare a Thumb War.*
> *Five, six, seven, eight,*
> *Try to keep your thumb straight.*
> *Nine, ten, let's begin!*

Get Your Game Face On

The thumb is the perfect canvas for expression, individualization, and awesomeness—all you need is a marker! Here are some character ideas to get you pumped up:

   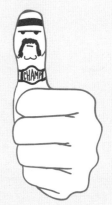

THE LUCHA THUMBRE   THE OPPOSABLE SHARK   THE DIGIT NINJA   THE SUPER-PHALANGE

FINGER JOUSTING
A New Finger-to-Finger Fighting Classic

Game Stats

STYLE: Close combat game

PLAYERS: Two

REQUIREMENTS:
Two hands
Two extended index fingers

SKILLS:
Hand-eye coordination
Arm strength
Finger strength

- - - - - - - - - - - -

ALSO KNOWN AS
Finger Fencing
Finger Duel
Russian Finger Fencing

WHAT IT IS
What do you get when you combine arm wrestling, fencing, and jousting but remove the weaponry; and then remove the horses, too—and then add a splash of wrestling? (We'll wait while you do the math.) The answer is Finger Jousting. While it's not a household name (yet) it's a perfect addition to the long and storied history of hand battle games.

WHAT'S THE POINT?
Simply put, the goal is to poke your opponent with your pointer finger. Less simply put, the goal is to treat your index finger like a lance in which you must make contact with your opponent's body in any designated area to score. Recommended match play consists of three rounds, each two minutes in length.

HOW YOU PLAY
1 Choose your opponent
Finger Jousting is played between two well-matched and worthy combatants. While it's not always possible, the competitors should be of similar size and build to make for the most balanced battle.

2 Begin with a gesture of good disposition
Don't let the combat metaphors fool you. Finger Jousting is a game for gentlemen and gentlewomen to behave ungently. It is tradition to establish sportsmanship with a positive gesture like a bow, handshake, or fist bump.

3 Grip hands, take stance
The jousters then grasp their opponent's right hand with their right hand, similar to an arm wrestling grip. Since the whole game relies on a solid grip between competitors, it's critical that they take the time to align their hands just so.

4 **Extend lances**

The match begins once the index finger of each person's right hand has been extended. If there is a mediator, it can start at his signal. If there is no mediator, it can start when competitors count down together: "Three, two, one . . . JOUST!"

5 **Commence the battle**

Keeping their right hands clasped, jousters use any technique they can to touch their pointed right index finger against their opponent's body. Jousters are not allowed to use their feet or latent (left) arm in an offensive manner; they may only be used for dodging and stability.

6 **Poke for points**

There are two primary ways to score a match:

A QUICK PLAY— any legal spot on the body counts as one point. A quick play match is usually played to one point.

B POINT PLAY—different parts of the body count for different amounts of points. The legs and latent arm count as one point. The chest, back, and neck count as two points. The head counts as three points. Point play matches are played to six points.

7 **Avoid fouls**

The first foul results in a warning. The second foul results in a second warning (if it's a quick play game) or loss of one point (if it's a Point Play game). The third offense results in automatic disqualification. Following are the most common fouls: **(a)** using feet or latent arm in an offensive manner; **(b)** separating jousting hands (if it cannot be determined who caused the separation, it is a warning); **(c)** sheathing of your lance (retracting your index finger mid-match); and **(d)** lancing the opponent's lancing arm—usually her right shoulder.

8 **End with a gesture of good disposition**

Finger Jousting should start and end with class. Again, consider a traditional bow, a hearty handshake or, if the match was particularly challenging, a classic "bro-hug."

SAFETY PATROL: This is the perfect instance to remind everyone that it is, in fact, all fun and games until someone gets poked in the eye. So please, keep your fingers out of your opponent's face.

JOUSTING TECHNIQUES

Majigger

A majigger is where a player rotates his lancing elbow counterclockwise toward the opponent's outside while moving his hand down. This allows the jouster to have a clear, open shot at lancing the lower body and pulls the opponent off balance.

Reverse Majigger

In this move, a player rotates his lancing elbow clockwise toward the opponent's body while moving his hand down. This allows the jouster to use an opponent's majigger against him to get a shot at the lower body or across the chest during a full reversal.

Bobbo Lance

A straight jousting move wherein a player cocks his right elbow back toward his chest pulling the opponent closer. The player then rapidly shoots out his arm, lancing the opponent in the chest or head.

Segal Slam

A judo-inspired move wherein a jouster rotates his back counterclockwise toward a charging opponent, bends over, and flips the opponent over the lancing shoulder to his back.

WORLD OF PLAY

In rural Germany, Finger-hakeln, also known as Alps Finger Wrestling, is a serious sport. Like Arm Wrestling, players face each other over a small table. They hook their middle fingers through a leather band and then attempt to pull the other player over the table.

Coach Says . . .

Finger Jousting works best when both players have the same dominant arm. If you are a lefty, you need to either strengthen up your righty game, or find another lefty to battle.

Insider Secrets: Finger Jousting

Finger jousting may seem like a game of luck and fingernails, but according to Julian Gluck, President of the World Finger Jousting Federation, the key to success in this cutthroat, combative sport, is mastering the four quadrants: **(1)** quickness, **(2)** strength, **(3)** technique, and **(4)** tradition. To achieve any success in the semiprofessional arena, you have to internalize these fundamental principles to perfect your own style.

QUICKNESS

According to Gluck, lightning-fast reflexes and cobra-like speed are instrumental to becoming a champion. He suggests earning points by rapidly rotating your lancing arm when your opponent's leg or latent arm is in reach, or by jetting forward when your assailant becomes fatigued. "Although you may not use your feet in an offensive manner, quick legwork will aid in dodging your antagonist's attacks and avoiding an errant lance," he suggests.

STRENGTH

Nobody ever said Finger Jousting is for the lazy. Gluck suggests maintaining a fitness regimen will help you pummel participating couch potatoes and keep your rival's index finger at bay. "I recommend introducing one-handed push-ups into your routine, doing them with one-finger if you're either gutsy or a Shaolin monk," he says. If finger push-ups are a little intense for you, try working with a pair of vice grips instead.

TECHNIQUE

If you want to gain the kind of Finger Jousting skills that will pay the bills, Gluck suggests you increase your repertoire of moves by mastering the elementary tactics, then progressing to more expert maneuvers. "My personal favorite is the spin majigger, wherein you rotate your body under your lancing arm toward your opponent's body, putting you in a momentarily inverted position in order to close the gap, granting the opportunity to gain an unexpected victory."

TRADITION

Gluck stresses that, first and foremost, Finger Jousting is a sport for gentlemen and gentlewomen. Begin each battle with a gesture of good disposition, such as a firm handshake or bow. "Without decorum, knights would be merely weaponized agents in a feudal bureaucracy astride horses," Gluck says. "By respecting your opponent and yourself, you can reach phalangelic harmony."

Julian Gluck is the founder and President of the World Finger Jousting Federation. For more information visit FingerJoust.com

CLAPPING GAMES
Play Along with Miss Marry, Miss Susie, and Godzilla

Game Stats

STYLE: Close combat game

PLAYERS: Two

REQUIREMENTS: Hands

SKILLS:

A sense of rhythm

Memory

Singing

Coordination

WHAT IT IS

Not all games during recess are competitive. Take clapping games: these classics are best when both participants play along together. Yes, cooperation! It sounds like a foreign word on the competitive playground, but just give it try. By doing so you'll be joining a long tradition in cultures around the world that have created and passed down these games. Anyone can enjoy them and jump right in with their besties, and with a little help from some handy instructions.

WHAT'S THE POINT

The point is simply to have fun together. There is no keeping score, no losers, but—you guessed it—there *are* plenty of winners. There is a timeless joy of creating music together and learning ever more complicated patterns and songs. If anything, the point is to share it with others.

HOW YOU PLAY

1 Find a partner

Again unlike other games, a partnership in hand clapping often lasts longer than just recess. It becomes a relationship as you two learn, practice, and ultimately master the different songs and clapping patterns.

2 Pick your distance

While it might seem like second nature, players must ensure they are the right distance apart. Too close and you won't connect properly on the claps—and risk violating personal space. Too far and you need to reach to connect, again, reducing the effectiveness of the clap.

3 Practice, practice, shimmy bop

These clapping games are more fun the faster they are played. So when players learn the patterns and practice often, over time they will gain speed and more fun.

HAND CLAPPING VARIATIONS
Miss Mary
(a.k.a. Miss Mary Mack, Mary Mack)
Considered the most common hand-clapping game in the English-speaking world, variations of Miss Mary have been played across the United States, throughout the United Kingdom, in New Zealand, and beyond.

The same clapping pattern is repeated for each verse. Skilled clappers can increase their speed to show off their dexterity and rhythm.

Miss Mary Mack, Mack, Mack,
All dressed in black, black, black,
With silver buttons, buttons, buttons,
All down her back, back, back.
She asked her mother, mother, mother,
For fifty cents, cents, cents,
To see the elephant, elephant, elephant.
Jump over the fence, fence, fence.
He jumped so high, high, high,
He reached the sky, sky, sky,
And he never came back, back, back,
'Till the end of July, 'ly, 'ly.

FUN FACT
The meaning of this song is the topic of much debate. Some think the first verse is a riddle leading to the word "coffin." Others think it secretly refers to the Merrimac, the Confederate battleship. We think it's about a gothy young woman and a very athletic elephant.

 1 Cross your arms on your chest —"Miss"

 2 Pat your thighs — "Mar"

 3 Clap your hands — "Y"

 4 Clap your right palm with your partner's — "Mack!"

 5 Clap your own hands.

 6 Clap your left palm with your partner's — "Mack!"

 7 Clap your own hands.

 8 Clap your right palm with your partner's — "Mack!"

 9 Clap your own hands.

(Repeat for each line)

Miss Susie
(a.k.a. Hello Operator, Miss Susie Had a Steamboat)

This American schoolyard game is imaginative, playful, and tantalizingly close to being crude. Naughty words are implied throughout, before the next verses reveal them to be quite safe after all. This is not surprising since it is a more kid-friendly version of a British Army marching cadence that is, well, not so polite.

FUN FACT

The bra has been known to be quoted as 40 acre as well.

Miss Susie had a steamboat,
The steamboat had a bell
(Ding-Ding)

Miss Susie went to heaven, the steamboat went to
Hello operator, please give me number nine
And if you disconnect me I'll chop off your
Behind the 'frigerator, there laid a piece of glass.
Miss Susie sat upon it, And cut her little
Ask me no more questions, please tell me no more lies.
The boys are in the bathroom, zipping up their
Flies are in the meadow, the bees are in the park.
Miss Susie and her boyfriend, are kissing in the D-A-R-K—(Dark! Dark!)

Dark is like a movie, a movie's like a show.
A show is like a TV screen
And that is all I know, I know my ma,
I know I know my pa,
I know I know my sister
With the 80 acre bra
My ma is Godzilla,
My pa is King Kong.
My sister is the stupid one
That taught me this dumb song.

1 "Miss" — clap your hands.

2 "Susie" — clap your partner's right hand.

3 "Had a" — clap your hands.

4 "Steamboat" — clap your partner's left hand.

Repeat these steps every line and make sure to keep the same beat and speed as your partner.

Pause on (Ding-Ding) and (Dark! Dark!) clap both your partner's hands.

Double, Double

No one wants to settle for a single when a double is better. A double of what you ask? Well, we don't know, but what do know is that more is better.

Double double this this,
Double double that that,
Double this, double that,
Double double this that.

1 On every "Double" — tap your partner's knuckles.

2 On every "This" — clap hands with your partner.

3 On every "That" — slap the back of your hands with your partner's.

Bim Bum

This clapping game is often performed with participants facing the same direction—instead of facing each other. It's a simple escalation game where in each round, the speed is increased—until you're clapping and snapping your bim bum off.

Bim bum,
Biddy biddy bum,
Biddy bum,
Biddy biddy bum,
Bim bum.
(Repeat)

Bim bum, bim bum,
Biddy biddy bum,
Biddy bum,
Biddy biddy bum,
Bim bum.
(Repeat)

1 On every "Bim" — clap your hands.

2 On every "Bum" — snap your fingers.

3 On every "Biddy" — pat your thighs.

Boom Snap Clap

This contemporary game should be called Boom Sass Rap because of its large doses of sassiness and sophisticated rhythm patterns. But that would be a terrible name for a terrifically contagious game.

Boom, Snap, Clap
Ba-Boom, Snap, Clap, Snap
Boom, Snap, Clap
Ba-Boom, Snap, Shh!

This is the basic routine:

WORLD OF PLAY

Ampe is a popular game from Ghana that combines clapping, jumping, and a bit of Rock-Paper-Scissors. The most basic version requires two players who perform a quick jump and clap sequence and then each stick out a leg at random. Depending on whether the legs are the same or opposite, one player earns a point with each series.

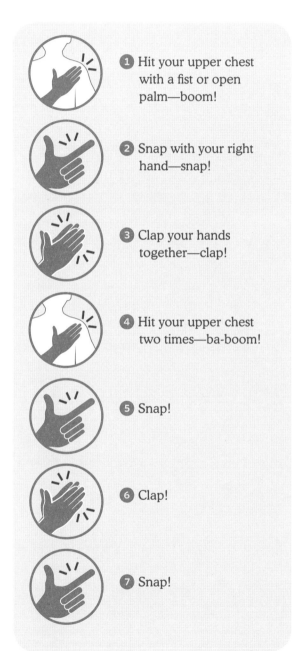

1. Hit your upper chest with a fist or open palm—boom!

2. Snap with your right hand—snap!

3. Clap your hands together—clap!

4. Hit your upper chest two times—ba-boom!

5. Snap!

6. Clap!

7. Snap!

8 Hit your chest—boom!

 9 Snap!

 10 Clap!

 11 Hit your chest twice again—ba-boom!

 12 Snap!

 13 Put your right finger to your mouth—shh!

Put it all together, doing the motions in-sync—boom, snap, clap. Ba-boom, snap, clap, snap. Boom, snap, clap. Ba-boom, snap, shh!

After you learn the basic routine, it's time to master all the variations.

1 Use only your right hand.

2 Use only your left hand.

3 Use both hands at the same time.

4 Cross your arms and use both your hands.

5 Use only your right hand but clap with your left foot.

6 Use only your left hand but clap with your right foot.

FUN FACT

Is there a clapping game gene? There might be. Research shows that children around the world naturally start inventing clapping games around age seven.

CIRCLE GAME
What's That over There? Made You Look!

Game Stats

STYLE: Deception game
PLAYERS: Two or more
REQUIREMENTS:
Index finger
Opposable thumb
Loads of time to kill
SKILLS:
Patience
Excellent peripheral vision
Ability to give and take
  a punch

- - - - - - - - - - - - -

ALSO KNOWN AS
Made You Look
Hand Circle Game
Hole-Tempting Game
Poke a Hole

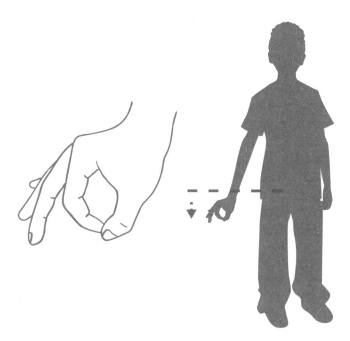

WHAT IT IS
When the going gets bored, the bored get punching. That's a pretty simple way to describe the Circle Game, a game that is a masterpiece of balanced boredom, subtle subterfuge, and well-placed punches. While not terribly complex, the Circle Game hinges on one founding principal—if you can trick someone into looking where they're not supposed to, then you get to punch them. If only all of life's scenarios were so easy to solve.

WHAT'S THE POINT?
The goal is to get another person, the looker, to stare directly at the circle you're making with your index finger and thumb. If the looker looks, you punish him accordingly with a punch or two. This is a free-flowing game that can go on

for multiple days and even years. It is not yet known how to respectably end a match—a player may need to throw a temper tantrum and demand that the game is over, forfeiting his dignity, but regaining his freedom.

HOW YOU PLAY

1 Make the Circle

Unlike most games, there's no official start to the Circle Game. Instead, a game begins the second a player decides to make a finger circle in hopes that another player will become a looker. To do this, the player connects the tips of his index finger and thumb to make a circle. The circle must then be placed somewhere below the player's waist height.

2 Make Them Look

The trick of the game is to get another person to not only notice your finger circle, but to also look into it. This can be done in a number of ways, as long as the finger circle never rises above the player's waist.

3 Punish with Punches

If someone manages to look directly into the finger circle, the player is allowed to punish them by administering a quick punch to the arm.

4 Index Finger Retaliation

If a looker manages to see the circle without directly looking at it, he has the option to poke throw the circle with his index finger. If he manages to do this successfully without actually looking at the circle, the looker gets to punch the other player twice.

5 Wipe It Clean

No matter which person delivers the final punches, the round isn't over until the player doing the punching, with his hand quickly brushes off the area he just punched on the looker. If the player does not wipe off the punch, he will then receive a punch himself.

ADDITIONAL RULES

- While different lures and distractions are allowed, the player making the circle is *not* allowed to force the circle into the other player's view.

- If a player attempts to thwart a circle with his finger, the finger must go through the circle without touching the sides of the circle. If it touches the sides of the circle at all, the player with the circle gets to punch.

- Poking through a circle *must be* done with an index finger—using any other fingers or objects results in additional punches.

DISTRACTION TECHNIQUES

Fake Knee Injury

Cringe and whine while gripping your knee in pretend pain. When a concerned sucker comes over to help, you can return their kindness with a deep look into the void of your finger circle!

Is This Gum on My Pants?

By appealing to the gum-related curiosity of bystanders, you can easily trick them into taking a gander at your finger circle.

Tying the Shoe

For some reason, when someone stops to tie their shoe, everyone else stops to watch them tie it. Reward their curiosity with a finger circle and some punches.

Hand Off

Whoever said you could only keep a finger circle on just your body? If you're in close quarters with others, sneak the circle onto another person's hip. When they look to see what's touching them, their eyes will sink right into the circle.

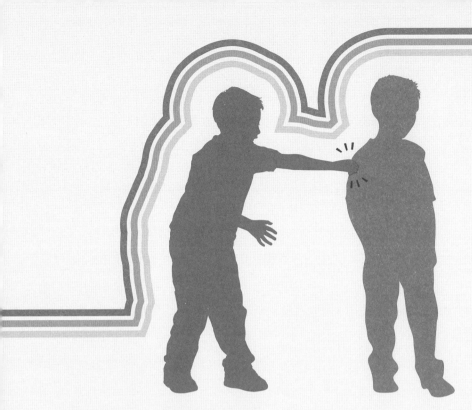

How to Punch a Friend

A punch delivered in a friendly game is very different than one delivered in an unfriendly brawl—well, almost. The goal of a friendly punch—also known as a buddy hit—is to inflict a small dose of pain, with no damage or bruising, and maximum embarrassment.

1 DRAW ATTENTION - Make sure to get the attention of others in the area to get the most social shaming as possible.

2 AIM FOR THE MEAT - The most acceptable and classy place to hit a friend is in the meaty part of their shoulder—professionally known as the deltoid.

3 AVOID DRAW BACKS - Winding up a throwing a haymaker is considered unfriendly. Keep your upper arm still while extending your forearm like you are using a hammer.

4 ALWAYS WIPE - As noted, it is both polite and Circle Game protocol to wipe the area you just punched.

Coach Says . . .

These top five "made you look" lines are proven to get you punching in no time.
1. Does this look swollen?
2. Look at this bug I caught outside.
3. Is this your money?
4. Is this your monkey?
5. What's this circle thing called?

OTHER WAYS TO PLAY

Finger Catch

The looker tries to put his finger in the circle, but the player with the circle is able to catch the looker's finger and grab hold of it. The looker gets punched three times.

Missed Poke

If the looker attempts to insert a finger but misses, he must touch his ear and say, "Ear to Clear." If he doesn't do this immediately after the miss, he will receive a punch.

Circle Break

The looker is able to not just insert a finger in the player's circle, but is also able to break it. The looker gets to punch the other player five times.

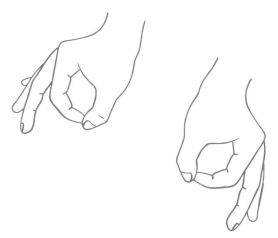

Two Circles

If the circle player gets the looker to look at two finger circles, he gets to give two punches.

Immunity Goggles

If a looker is able to don finger goggles—by placing his hands on his head as shown—then he is able to look directly at any circles without the risk of being punched.

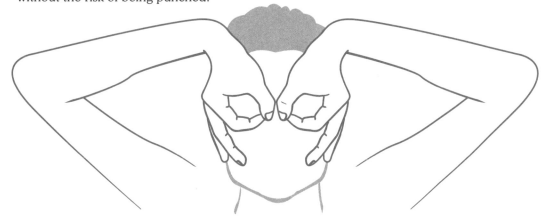

2

DEXTERITY & MENTAL GAMES

Big Fun Comes in Small Packages

Play is the highest form of research.
— **Albert Einstein**

Not every contest involves a cloud-reaching bounce, a side-splitting hit, or even leaving your house. Sometimes the smaller games pack in big fun. The games in this section won't cause you to break a sweat—unless it's from racking your brain to come up with a winning strategy. These activities are great for players of all abilities and have the added benefit of being both indoor and outdoor friendly—so say goodbye to rainy day boredom.

PENCIL FIGHTING
A War of Wood and Lead

Game Stats

STYLE: Combat game

PLAYERS: Two

REQUIREMENTS:

Two pencils of equal size,
one for each player

SKILLS:

Strong wrists

Tough hands

A good grip

Masterful pencil-pushing
abilities

- - - - - - - - - -

ALSO KNOWN AS

Pencil Break

Pencil Pop

Pencil Duel

WHAT IT IS

Pencil fighting combines the grit of a sword fight, the tension of a duel, and the supplies of a stationery closet—all combined into an epic battle between two fierce competitors. Two players take turns attacking each other's pencil. As the fight goes on, it's up to each player to deliver blow upon devastating blow to the other players pencil until it breaks.

WHAT'S THE POINT?

Whoever breaks the other person's pencil first is the ultimate pencil champion (at least until the next game).

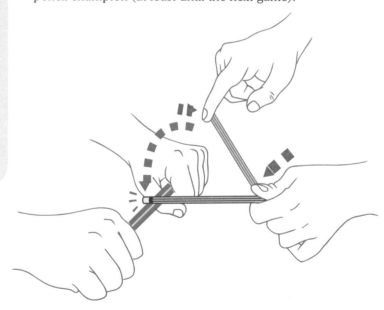

HOW YOU PLAY

1 Choose your weapon

Each player picks a pencil of his or her choice. However, both players must agree upon their chosen weapon, so if one player feels that the other player's pencil gives an unfair advantage, they both must choose another.

② Determine Firsts

Of course, any of the traditional methods on page 14 will serve for this purpose. However, if you really want to get into the spirit, flip a pink pearl eraser and call a side like you would for a coin toss.

③ Establish the strikee hold

The game starts with one player, the strikee, holding her pencil parallel to the ground, gripping it with both hands at each end with clenched fists. Thumbs cannot be extended to provide extra bracing support. There must be a least two and a half inches of exposed, hittable wood between the player's hands. If playing with a hexagonal pencil, one of the flat sides of the pencil must be facing upward.

④ Establish the striker strike

The other player, the striker, holds the pencil so that it is perpendicular with the strikee's pencil. Holding the pencil at both ends with both hands, the attacker pulls back the top portion (most commonly the eraser end) of his pencil and releases, allowing the top to fire downward at the center of the defender's pencil. The striker's bottom hand must stay mostly stationary, so that the power comes from the snapping action.

⑤ Penalty strikes

While generally considered a no-holds-barred melee, there are still a few cases in which a violating player must give up an extra strike from their opponent: **(a)** dropping the pencil at any time during the match, **(b)** intentionally hitting an opponent on the fingers, **(c)** whiffing or otherwise not connecting on a strike, **(d)** flinching before a hit, if in the position of the strikee.

⑥ The counter attack

If on the first attack the striker fails to break the pencil of the strikee, the roles are reversed and the strikee now becomes the striker. This back and forth keeps going, until there is breakage.

SAFETY PATROL: Shards of wood and graphite can fly anywhere. And by anywhere we mean your eyes. So be careful!

FUN FACT

The origins of pencil fighting are generally traced back to the opulent 1980s, the height of the "me" generation and frivolous spending—making the wasteful nature of the game quite understandable.

7 Breakage

The match is over when one of the pencils breaks completely into two pieces. In most cases it is the pencil being hit, but the striker's pencil is likely to shatter during a match as well.

If a pencil is cracked, but not fully broken in two, an impartial spectator may determine if the match can continue. If on the off chance both pencils break at the exact same time, the striker gets the win.

EXPERT STRATEGIES

Receiving the Strike

Strikees can reduce the damage inflicted by softening the blow. Without moving your hands, which would result in a penalty strike, you can loosen your grip slightly to allow your hands to act as shock absorbers.

Delivering a Killer Strike

Strikers can increase their chance of breakage by taking a cue from karate experts. Aim past your opponent's pencil to ensure you will follow through with as much force as possible. This increases your speed at contact and will likely cause more damage to the competing pencil.

OPTIONAL RULES

For a game that has grown solely through the underground recess and hallway gaming circuit, it is surprising that there are not more variations in game play. That said, here are the biggest variations in rules.

Pencil Policy

Some purists believe that the game is a best played with identical pencils—if possible freshly pulled from the same box—to ensure a level no. 2 playing field.

Unrestricted Equipment

Others approach the game more like a monster truck competition and encourage customization and creativity in pencil development like coating your pencil with nail polish lacquer for extra support or flattening the eraser to create an "axe" with the metal shaft.

FUN FACT

Thanks to the Seattle-based World Extreme Pencil Fighting League (WXPFL), Pencil Fighting has gone pro. They add the theatrics of professional wrestling with the fury and competition of pencil fighting—the actual pencil fights are real and unscripted.

Unrestricted Striking

There are some who prefer to play a version that does not restrict the strike to the wrist snapping method. This opens up the door to a full body swing that greatly reduces the number of strikes to break.

No Turning

Some traditionalists believe that the strikee should not be allowed to rotate their pencil to present areas of less damage in attempt to stave off breakage.

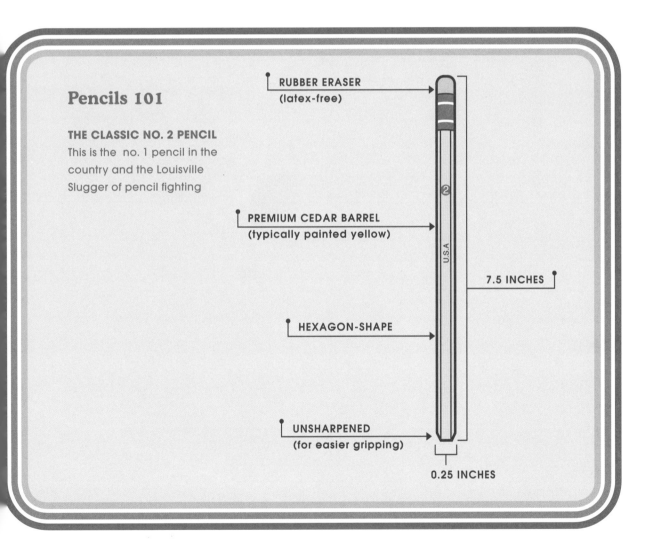

Pencils 101

THE CLASSIC NO. 2 PENCIL
This is the no. 1 pencil in the country and the Louisville Slugger of pencil fighting

RUBBER ERASER
(latex-free)

PREMIUM CEDAR BARREL
(typically painted yellow)

2

U.S.A

7.5 INCHES

HEXAGON-SHAPE

UNSHARPENED
(for easier gripping)

0.25 INCHES

COIN BASKETBALL
Shoot Some Hoops without Shooting or Hoops

Game Stats

STYLE: Digital Dexterity
PLAYERS: Two
REQUIREMENTS:
A large coin
A flat, smooth surface (a
    desk or table is perfect)
SKILLS:
Good hand-eye
    coordination
Fast fingers
Dunking skills

WHAT IT IS

Coin Basketball takes out all the hassle of basketball but leaves in all the hustle! In this pint-sized version of the original, players flick and spin a coin down the court in order to get it as close as possible to the other player's net (i.e., their hands) at the other end of the table. From there, they get some solo time on the court to show off their finger shooting skills and thumb dunking moves.

WHAT'S THE POINT?

Bring the coin up the court and either shoot or dunk to score. The first player to reach 5 points wins. Play-by-play color commentary is optional, but highly entertaining.

HOW YOU PLAY

1 Tip-off

Players flip a coin and call it in the air. Whoever gets it right gets Firsts and possession of the coin. Once this is decided, both players face each other across the table. The player who won the coin toss is on offense. He starts by putting the coin in front of him, directly on the edge of the table. Meanwhile, the player on defense must create the basket using his hands placed directly in front of him resting on the table.

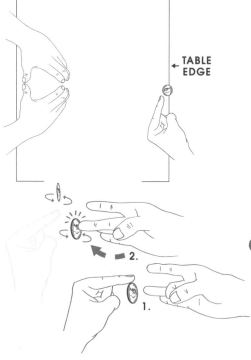

← TABLE
    EDGE

2 Take it up the court

The player on offense starts with an inbounds "pass" by spinning the coin toward the opponent's side of the table. If the coin goes off the table, the defending player gets a point.

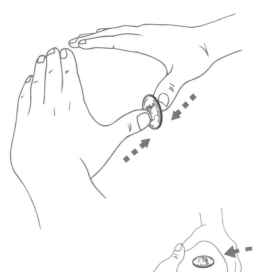

③ Catching the coin pass

The player on offense must then catch his own "pass," stopping the coin by pinning it between his thumbs. No other fingers can be used. If he is not able to catch it in an upright position, he loses possession. This requires the perfect timing since as the coin slows down it becomes harder to catch.

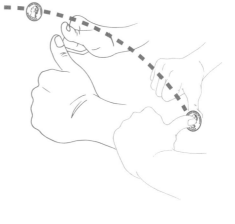

④ The shot

Now that the coin has been successfully caught and is trapped between the player's thumbs, he must set his "feet" by placing his knuckles down on the table. This is his shooting position. His knuckles must remain in contact with the table, but the rest of his hands can be used to flick the quarter into the defender's basket. If he is close enough, he can dunk it.

⑤ Keeping score

If the coin goes in the basket, the offensive player gets a point and is now on defense. If he misses, he returns to defense without a point. The first player to earn five points wins, though this game is often played until time runs out.

Coach Says . . .

Catching a coin at full speed is a risky move since you're more likely to fumble. Instead, do what I do, and wait for it to slow down, but stop it before it starts wobbling.

SPINNING TECHNIQUES
The Two-Hand Twist
This method uses both hands to provide the energy for the spin. The left hand uses the index and middle fingers together on one edge of the coin with the thumb of the right hand on the other. Pressure should be applied equally in both directions. When ready to spin, both hands shift slightly to release the coin in a counterclockwise spin. This technique delivers a reliable spin, but doesn't allow for the fastest rotation or very much directional force.

Flick Spin
Hold the coin upright with just your left index finger, then flick your right index finger quickly at the coin, providing both spin and directional force. This classic method has average consistency but it does provide more distance, which is perfect for Coin Basketball.

The One-Handed Flick Spin
This technique is all about show. Hold the coin upright with your right index finger. Then create a flick formation with your thumb and middle finger. When the middle finger is released it should produce a spin on par with a traditional flick spin, but gaining some extra style points.

OPTIONAL RULES
Out of Bounds
It is legal to use the opponent's body as a backboard to bank in a shot. If, however, the coin hits him above the neckline, it is considered out of bounds—even if it drops in the net.

Half-Court Defense
Some people allow the defender to play defense by placing his hand on the court before the offense tips off. They can't move their hand around, but if the coin touches their hand, possession switches.

Low Blows Allowed
It's controversial among serious Coin Basketball players, but some rules allow the offensive player to blow the spinning coin to influence path and location. It is not without some risks, though, since it might hinder an otherwise healthy spin.

FUN FACT
When a coin is done spinning and is wobbling low to the table, it is said by physicists to be *spolling*—part spinning and part rolling in place.

FINGER HOCKEY
The Coolest Sport on Ice, without the Ice

WHAT IT IS

Like Paper Football and Coin Basketball, this is yet another desk-friendly adaptation of a classic game, and a perfect solution for rainy day boredom. While the pace is decidedly slower than other games, the biggest benefit here is that the coin is unlikely to be launched into air and get lost or confiscated. So you get to play with your money—and keep it too.

WHAT'S THE POINT?

Finger Hockey is all about two things: flicking coins and scoring goals. Each player takes turns flicking the coins down the rink (a.k.a. the desk) until they manage to score a goal. The person with the most goals by the end of recess wins.

HOW YOU PLAY

1 The set-up

Players flip a coin and call it in the air. Whoever wins the toss gets the first possession. Once this is decided, both players face each other across the table. The player who won the coin toss is on offense. He then racks the coins up in the center of the desk in a triangle formation, with the single "point" of the formation facing the player on offense.

2 The face-off

The player on offense flicks the coin facing him so that it collides with the other two coins and sends them sliding over the desk. With the coins now scattered, it's the other player's turn to take offense. The first player now puts his hands flat on his edge of the desk, connecting his thumbs and making a U-shaped goal for the other player to aim.

Game Stats

PLAYERS: Two
STYLE: Digital Dexterity
REQUIREMENTS:
Three large coins of the
    same size
A flat, smooth surface (a
    desk or table is perfect)
At least two hands
SKILLS:
Hand-eye coordination
Deft sliding skills

- - - - - - - - - -

ALSO KNOWN AS
3-Coin Hockey
Coin Hockey
Quarter Hockey

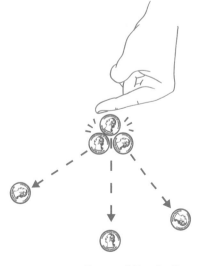

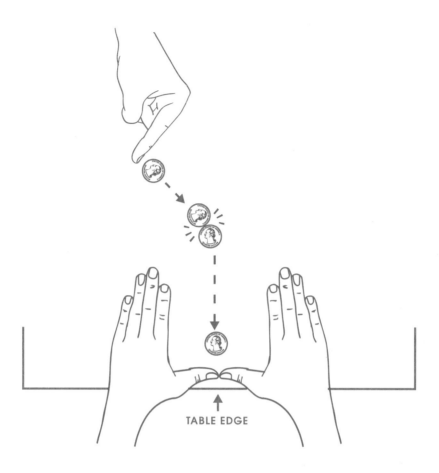

TABLE EDGE

❸ Shoot it up the ice

The second player, now on offense, must flick the coin closest to him, aiming for it to collide with one or more of the other coins and move them closer to the goal. If he makes a coin into the goal, he gets a point! If he doesn't, it's the other player's turn again.

❹ Play some D

The players continue to take turns trying to flick a coin so that it pushes another coin into the goal. A player can either try to go for the goal, or he can play defense and attempt to knock coins away from his goal. Each time a player scores a goal, however, the coins must be re-centered in the triangle formation again. The player who scored the goal then gets to start the next round.

ADDITIONAL RULES

- A goal only counts if it was knocked into the goal by another coin

- Players are not allowed to reset coins until a goal is scored

- If a player knocks any of the coins off of the desk, the other player gets to reset the coins and gets a new turn

- Coins must always be flicked—pushing, sliding, or moving a coin in any other way is forbidden

- When it's not a player's turn, that player must have his hands in goal post formation. If he doesn't, it's an extra turn for the other player

OTHER WAYS TO PLAY

In-Betweeners

This variation adds a little more challenge and skill to the game. Instead of using a coin to knock other coins down the ice, the player must slide a coin between the other two coins for a move to count. This makes it that much harder to navigate toward the goal and can add a fun challenge to those who have already conquered the traditional version of the game.

Mini-Goals

Instead of using both hands to make a big ol' wide-open goal for your opponent, try playing with mini goals. Do this by taking one hand and sticking the index and pinky fingers out, while pushing your middle and ring fingers up against the desk. This makes for a much smaller, more challenging goal to aim for. Spice things up by using both hands to make this goal, assigning different point values to each one.

PAPER FOOTBALL
America's Game, Only Smaller ... and Slower

Game Stats

PLAYERS: Two
STYLE: Digital Dexterity
REQUIREMENTS:

One 8.5 x 11 inch piece
of paper

A flat, smooth surface (a
desk or table is perfect)

SKILLS:

Folding skills

Good depth perception

Strong flicking ability

- - - - - - - - - - -

ALSO KNOWN AS

Finger Football

Chinese Football

Flick Football

Tabletop Football

WHAT IT IS
Paper Football takes all the fun, excitement, and drama of the gridiron classic and folds it into the smaller confines of a simple desk. It's played with nothing more than a piece of paper, a desk, and some thumbs and fingers. There are few games in the world that match the tension, frustration, and ultimately, the triumph found in lining up a perfect field goal and landing it squarely between the other player's goal post, er, thumbs.

WHAT'S THE POINT?
Just like with regular football, the goal of Paper Football is to get your ball into the other player's end zone in order to score points in one of two ways: **(a)** a touchdown or **(b)** a field goal. The first player to score twenty-one points takes the game and the glory!

HOW YOU PLAY
1 **The "coin" toss**
Players mark an "X" on one side of the ball and flip the ball into the air. While in the air, one player calls "X" or "No X," whoever calls correctly gets to choose whether to kick off or receive the ball.

2 **The kickoff**
Both players take opposite sides of the field (a.k.a. the desk). The player who is performing the kickoff sets the ball up by standing the ball on a corner and holding it up under a fingertip of one hand while using the other hand to flick (or kick) the ball toward the opposing player's end of the table. Wherever the ball lands is considered the spot where the other player (the receiver) begins his turn.

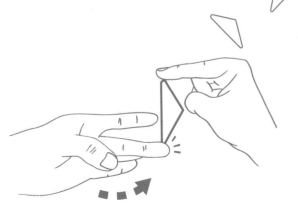

How to Make a Paper Football

Making a paper football is as easy as finding a regular piece of 8½" × 11" paper. So grab a sheet and follow these simple steps to create your own paper pigskin.

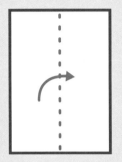

FOLD THE FLAT SHEET IN HALF

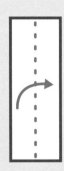

FOLD IN HALF AGAIN

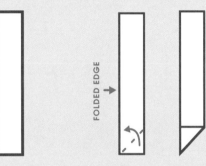

FOLDED EDGE →

FOLD OVER LOWER CORNER OPENING

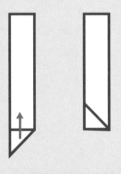

NOW FOLD THE NEW CORNER STRAIGHT UP

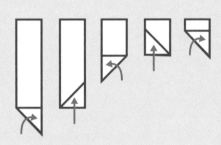

ALTERNATE AND REPEAT FOLDING THE CORNERS 5 MORE TIMES

FOLD THE TOP CORNERS IN FOR THE TUCK

TUCK THE TOP EDGE DOWN INTO THE FOOTBALL'S OPENING

Coach Says . . .

When setting up for a flick, make sure you hold the football upright with the tip pointing toward the direction you want it to fly.

③ The return

From where the ball landed, the receiver has four chances (or "downs") to move the ball back up the field and across the kicker's end zone—the far edge of the table. The receiver does this by flicking the ball so that it slides across the desk.

④ Touchdown!

If the receiver can get any part of the ball to stick out across the end zone within four turns, that's a touchdown, which is awarded six points. After scoring a touchdown, he has the option of kicking for an extra point. This is performed the same way as a kickoff is, however, the ball must fly through the goal post, which is created by the other player who is pushing his thumb tips together while raising his index fingers to the air. If he makes the shot, he gets an extra point.

⑤ Field goal!

If the receiver can't get a touchdown within four downs, then he must take a field goal—that is, he must kick the ball from the last spot it landed. Again, he's aiming at the goal post created by the other player. If a player makes a field goal, he is awarded three points.

⑥ Turnover!

If the receiver can't make a touchdown, a field goal, or if the ball goes off any edge of the table, the ball goes to the other player, who now assumes the role of the receiver. The ball is placed on the approximate spot where the last flick happened.

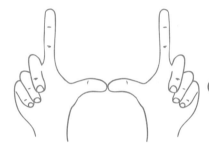

OPTIONAL RULES

The One Touch Rule

Doing any more than a simple flick while moving the ball up field—for instance, double flicking, sliding the ball, or doing anything else other than a simple flick—can result in having a down removed.

No Kick Interference

Interfering moves, such as blocking the ball with your hand or moving the goal posts, can result in the other player being granted additional downs.

SAFETY PATROL: It's almost impossible to mention Paper Football without mentioning all the poor souls who suffer each year from projectile eye pokes (PEP). There's no shame in closing or covering your eyes if a paper football is rocketing toward your face. Doing so can protect you from becoming another victim of PEP!

No Over Kicking

Rekicking the ball on a kickoff is a penalty and automatically grants the receiver the opportunity to start a quarter of the way up the field.

OTHER WAYS TO PLAY

Kicker's Game

In this quicker, simplified variation of the game, players only kick the ball back and forth, attempting to score points by getting the ball through the other player's goal posts. Each goal counts for one point, and the player to make it to six points, or whoever has the most points at the end of a set amount of time, wins.

Strikes

In this version, players are allowed only one chance to move the ball forward (as opposed to four downs). If the player goes too far and accidentally pushes the ball off of the opponent's end of the able, they get a strike. Once a player has three strikes against them, the other player receives a free field goal.

Quarters

This noisier, more challenging variation of the game uses a quarter instead of a paper football. The rules are almost the same, however, the player must move the ball up the field by keeping it spinning with a series of gentle flicks. Instead of kicking the ball through on field goals and extra points, the player is required to push the coin through by sliding it with his thumb.

Coach Says . . .

When you position your flick for the kick, make sure your index finger is tilted back just slightly and then fire away, aiming to hit the ball toward the bottom. If done right, the ball should fly upward in a perfect arc on a flight path to victory.

MARBLES
Knuckling Down with One of the Oldest Games in the World

WHAT IT IS

Don't let the low-tech equipment fool you: marbles is the original addictive social game. The point of the game is to shoot your marbles and knock away your opponent's—sometimes for keeps (to build a killer collection) and sometimes just for fun. Either way, there are tons of variations and formats to play in, so these little guys never get old.

Marbles 101

EQUIPMENT

Most of today's marbles are made from glass through various processes. Some are collectable works of art, some are just playthings. But what remains constant are the two main types of marbles.

½ to ⅝ inch marbles
a.k.a. ducks, mibs, kimmies, alleys
¾ to 1 inch shooters
a.k.a. taw, knuckler, aggie, moonie, boss

↑ ½–⅝ INCH

¾–1 INCH ↑

REGULAR   **SHOOTER**

These different size marbles can come in a variety of designs. Following are a few of the most common ones:

CAT'S EYES—clear marbles streaked with different-colored vanes inside

CLOUDS—colored flecks of glass that look like clouds floating over the core

ONION SKINS—colored flecks of glass are stretched to create a pattern like an onion

MARBLES TECHNIQUES

While there are a lot of different ways to play Marbles, there are some rules and techniques that are consistent throughout each variation. These standardized rules and regulations make Marbles kind of unique among recess games because it's one of the few games where the rules remain the same no matter where you go.

Knuckling Down

The knuckle down technique is like the baseball swing of Marbles—it's how you play offense and can dictate how you win the game. Knuckling down is simple—take a marble (usually a shooter, but not always) and wrap your index finger around it. Then, place the knuckle of your index finger down onto the floor, aiming the marble at your target. When you're ready to shoot, use your thumb to flick the marble out of your index finger so it goes flying into its target.

WORLD OF PLAY

Marbles as we know them— the small, clear balls made out of glass, ceramic, or acrylic—were invented in Germany in the 1800s. However, early versions of this popular game have been found in almost every ancient civilization. The Egyptians and Aztecs played with clay marbles, while the Greeks and Romans used round, polished nuts.

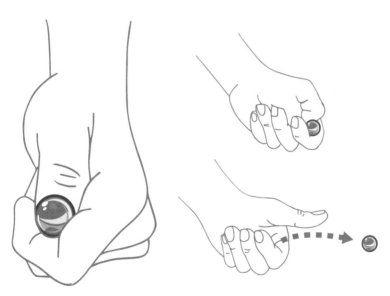

Surfaces

They say you can play marbles on any flat surface, which is true, but the type of surface can dramatically affect the game. If playing indoors on a floor or low-pile carpet, you'll need to use some string and tape to mark the boundary. Outdoors, a smooth dirt surface like a well-groomed baseball infield or clay tennis court is ideal since it controls the roll and you can mark directly on ground. If playing on blacktop or cement, you'll need chalk.

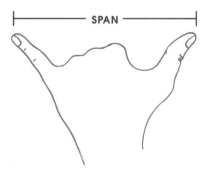

WORLD OF PLAY

In Thailand they play an elaborate version of Marbles called E-Gar Fuk Khai (crow sits on eggs), which starts with a circle drawn in the ground to represent the "nest" and hold the "eggs"—a pile of small marbles. One player is designated as the "crow" and the other as the "owner." The crow attempts to protect the eggs from being stolen by the other players. When all of the eggs have been stolen the crow is then blindfolded as the eggs are hidden around the area. Afterwards the crow removes the blindfold and looks for the missing eggs. The player who is the owner of the first egg to be found takes over the role as the crow.

Spans

A span is the measure of unit used in most games of Marbles. It's the distance from the tip of one's outstretched thumb to the tip of one's outstretched pinky. Since spans can be different depending on the size of the player's hand, it's important to keep track of whose turn it is to determine the span.

Firsts

In Marbles there is a very strict way of determining who goes first for each game. Before the game starts, players mark a line (often an existing boundary line like a seam in the carpet or a crack in the sidewalk). Each player takes turns knuckling down and shooting. Whoever gets their marble closest to the line without going over wins Firsts.

Keepsies and Friendlies

Before starting a game, players must first decide if they're playing keepsies or friendlies. Playing keepsies means that players get to keep any marbles they collect during the course of the game. Because the unique designs of marbles encourage collecting, keepsies can be a fun way of enhancing your marble collection with rare and interesting pieces. If you're not very good at Marbles and you're worried about losing your collection, it might be better to play friendlies, which means that all marbles go back to their original owners at the end of the game.

RINGER

In this classic variation of Marbles, players gather around a circle and try to knock out as many marbles as they can. If a player can knock a marble out of the ring, he gets to pick up the marble, which counts as one point. Whoever knocks out the most marbles at the end of the game is the winner.

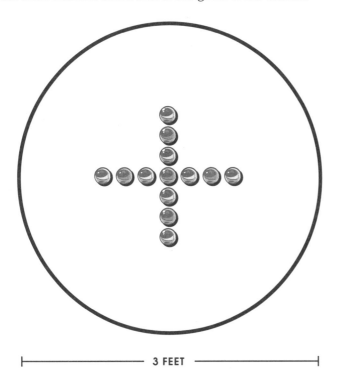

|—————————— 3 FEET ——————————|

Game Stats

PLAYERS: Two to four
REQUIREMENTS:
A shooter marble (one for each player)
An even number of marbles (each player should provide at least six)
Chalk (if you're outside) or a length of rope or tape long enough to make a 3-foot circle (if you're inside)

HOW YOU PLAY

1 Mark your territory
Using either chalk or a length or rope, create a circle with a three-foot diameter.

2 Marble up
In the center of the circle, line up the marbles so that they form a perfectly even plus sign.

3 Knuckle down
The first player picks a spot on the outside of the ring, knuckles down, and takes a shot at the marbles with her shooter. The goal is to knock one or more of the marbles outside of the ring.

4 Keep them rolling
If the player knocks a marble out of the ring, she picks it up, stashes it away, and knuckles down for the next shot from wherever her shooter landed. That player keeps going until she misses, then it's the next player's turn.

5 Count them out
Players keep going in order until all the marbles are knocked out of the ring. Whoever has the most marbles at the end is the winner.

Game Stats

PLAYERS: Two to four
REQUIREMENTS:
A shooter marble (one for each player)
An even number of marbles (each player should provide at least six)
Chalk (if you're outside) or four 18-inch lengths of rope or tape (if you're inside)

HOLEY BANG
This Marbles game combines bowling, golf, and digging to create one awesome event! Players each take turns rolling their marbles across the dirt toward a hole in the ground, trying to sink a hole in one.

HOW YOU PLAY
1 Can you dig it?
Find a smooth dirt patch that's at least 6 feet long (but the bigger the better). Dig a small, shallow hole in the ground, then mark a throw line roughly 6 feet away from it (you can make the line farther away if you want more of a challenge).

2 Hit the dirt
Each player takes turns knuckling down at the throw line, each trying to shoot their marbles into the hole.

3 He shoots, he scores!
When a player manages to land a marble in the hole, he gets to collect all the marbles that didn't make it into the hole. Players shoot until they have no more marbles left. Whoever has collected the most marbles wins.

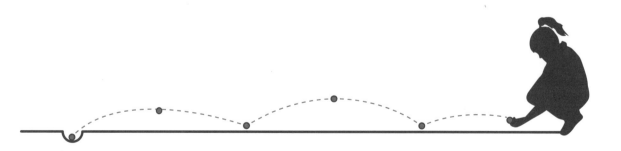

KNUCKLE BOX

This version of Marbles is a lot like Ringer, only a bit squarer—literally. Players take aim at other players' marbles, each trying to collect as many marbles as they can.

HOW YOU PLAY

1 **Square things off**

Create a square that has four even sides of 18 inches each. Then all the players throw their marbles into the square wherever they like.

2 **Span and shoot**

The first player picks a spot somewhere around the square and knuckles down one span inside the square, aiming to knock at least one marble out of the square.

3 **Shooter for grabs**

If the player manages to knock a marble and his shooter out of the square, he collects both and takes another shot. If he manages to just knock a marble out but his shooter remains in the square, he collects the marble but his shooter now becomes a target.

4 **The money ball**

If another player knocks out the first player's shooter, the first player must turn over all of his marbles to that player. If none of the other players manage to hit the shooter, the first player can spend his next turn picking up the shooter.

5 **Collect and win**

Players continue this until all of the original marbles have been knocked out of the square. Whoever has collected the most marbles at the end of the game wins.

Game Stats

PLAYERS: Two to four
REQUIREMENTS:
An even number of marbles
   (each player should
   provide at least six)
An outdoors dirt patch
A shallow hole dug into
   the dirt
A trowel, spoon, or flat stick
   (to dig the hole)

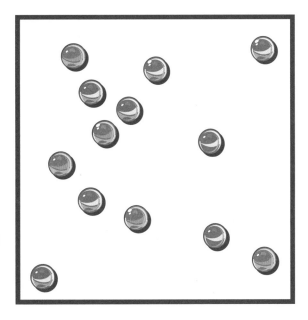

├─────────── **18 INCHES** ───────────┤

Game Stats

PLAYERS: Two to four
REQUIREMENTS:
A shooter marble (one for
    each player)
A clear, flat floor

BOUNCE ABOUT

Bounce About is not only an easy way to play Marbles, it's also an easy way to collect new ones as well. Players take turns tossing their marbles both in the air and at other players' marbles, hoping to knock them out of the air.

HOW YOU PLAY

1 Toss up

The first player takes his shooter and tosses it into the air, aiming roughly 5 feet in front of him. While his marble is in the air, the next player throws her shooter up, attempting to knock the first player's marble out of the air. As the second player's marble is in the air, the third player throws his and so on.

2 Keep 'em flying

Each player continues this cycle, throwing their shooter from the last spot that it landed until they hit one of the other players' shooters.

3 Keep or forfeit

If a player manages to hit another player's shooter in the air, they get to keep either the shooter or another marble from that player's kit. The choice is up to the player whose shooter was hit.

HUNDREDS

Hundreds is the ultimate one-on-one marble shootout. Two players agree on a spot for shooting and both try their best to get their marbles into the circle while making sure the other player doesn't.

HOW YOU PLAY

1 Create boundaries

Using chalk or length of rope, create a circle that is only 12 inches in diameter. From there, each player agrees on a shooting distance from the circle (3 spans is a good distance for beginners).

2 Shoot it out

Both players knuckle down and take a shot at the same time. The goal is to get your shooter to stop in the circle while making sure your opponent's shooter rolls out.

3 All or nothing

If both marbles stay in the circle or if both marbles roll out of the circle, neither player receives points. If a player manages to get her marble to stay in the circle while the other player's marble is outside of the circle, that player is awarded 10 points. First player to make it to 100 points wins.

JACKS
A Jacked-up Version of Knucklebones!

Game Stats

STYLE: Digital dexterity
PLAYERS: One to six
REQUIREMENTS:
One small rubber ball
Ten Jacks (a couple of
    spares couldn't hurt)
A flat, smooth surface (the
    sidewalk works well)
SKILLS:
Expert hand-eye
    coordination
Speedy hands
Monk-like patience

- - - - - - - - - -

ALSO KNOWN AS
Knucklebone
Hucklebone
Dibs
Chuckstones
Onsies
Jax

WHAT IT IS
Some may dismiss Jacks as being a bit old-fashioned, but those naysayers are missing out on a classic game steeped in history, skill, and a healthy dose of greed. Simply challenge yourself by seeing how many jacks you can grab before you have to catch the bouncing ball. But don't let these simple instructions fool you—while the game may sound easy, there are few games in life that can frustrate the clumsy and reward the skilled like Jacks does!

WHAT'S THE POINT?
Players are required to toss the ball into the air with one hand and, with that same hand, scoop up a predetermined amount of jacks before the ball has a chance to bounce more than once. The first player to complete all of the predetermined sequences wins!

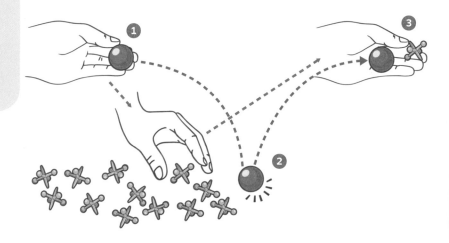

HOW YOU PLAY

1 **Tossing for Firsts**

Players begin by sitting across from each other or in a circle. Each player takes a turn resting all of the jacks on the back of their palm, quickly turning their palm over and trying to catch as many jacks as possible. In Jacks, this is known as *jockeying*. The player who catches the most jacks gets Firsts.

2 **Spilling the jacks**

The first player then collects all the jacks in both hands and lightly tosses them into the air. The objective is to get all the jacks to land in the center of all the players, preferably grouped close together.

3 **Onesies for the money**

The first player begins his turn by trying to go for onesies— that is, he has to throw the ball into the air with one hand and, with the same hand, collect one and only one jack, and then catch the ball after it bounces once and only once.

4 **Mistakes to take away your turn**

It's not as simple as just picking up a jack, it needs to be done correctly. And that means avoiding any of the following most common mistakes: **(a)** failing to pick up the correct number of jacks, **(b)** dropping or bobbling the jacks, **(c)** dropping or bobbling the ball, **(d)** bouncing the ball out of reach, and **(e)** accidently touching or tipping a jack.

If a player makes any of these errors, his turn is over and he will pick up at that number when it is his turn again.

5 **Twosies and beyond**

After a player is able to pick up all ten jacks one at a time, they move to the next round of twosies—picking up jacks two at a time. In some subsequent rounds, there will be left over jacks (threesies, foursies, fivesies, sixies, sevensies, eighties, and ninesies) that are picked up on the last throw.

6 **Big little wins**

The game continues on this path, with each player taking turns. The first player who completes every round all the way up to tensies wins.

FUN FACT
THE LEGENDARY GAME

In history, Jacks has turned up in both ancient Greece and Egypt, where players were known to compete using a wooden ball and knuckle bones from sheep. In fact, the game was originally referred to as "Knuckle-bones" for that very reason. Early records dating back to ancient Greece make mention of the game: there are tales of Zeus and other gods playing it. There are even documents that attribute the game as a creation of the Egyptians—supposedly handed down by the Egyptian god, Thoth. So better step up your game, mortals!

WORLD OF PLAY

Kudoda is a variation on Jacks from Zimbabwe. Players sit around a shallow dish full of small pebbles or marbles in the center and try to grab as many as they can between throws of another marble.

JACKS 101

A standard Jacks kit includes eleven pieces:

Ten plastic or metal jacks
  (¾ inch each)
One rubber ball (1 inch)
A cloth sack for storage

¾ INCH

1 INCH

JACK

BALL

Metal or Plastic?

While a newbie might not be too concerned with what
material their jacks are made of, some more advanced players may be wondering if it's worth spending a couple of extra
bucks on a set of metal jacks instead of plastic ones. The
answer depends on your preference.

Plastic jacks tend to be a little lighter. This can make things
slightly more difficult as the weight of the jack may make it
easier to accidentally sweep jacks around or errantly toss
them. The extra heft from the metal jacks mean they won't
drift around on the ground as easily if accidentally touched,
plus they may be slightly easier to toss from one hand to the
other during game play.

ADDITIONAL RULES

Here are some of the stricter rules of the game.

No Touching

If a player touches any jacks other than the ones he is trying to pick up, his turn is over.

No Double Dipping

If a player collects more jacks then he is supposed to during his turn, it's considered a foul and the player forfeits his turn.

No Bouncing

To make things extra difficult, players can invoke the rule that the ball must be caught before it bounces on the ground.

EXPERT STRATEGIES

Start Low

When bouncing the ball, start with your hand low to the ground and bounce from there. While the ball may not bounce as high, your hand will already be positioned low enough to scoop up some quick jacks.

Keep it Straight

The key is to keep the path of the ball as close to your original throwing position as possible so you don't need to chase after it. So toss the ball as straight and perpendicular to the ground as possible.

Don't Break Your Stride

Bouncing the ball, picking up the jacks, and catching the ball should be one fluid motion. Your hands should be approaching the jacks with a curved motion—creating a scoop not just a straight pickup.

Cover the Spread

When you first scatter the jacks onto the playing surface, try to scatter them evenly, not too close together or too far apart.

FUN FACT
JOCKEYING THE TAW

Back in the day, in a time when rubber balls weren't easily purchased with a quarter at the toy store, scrounging up the proper equipment for a game of Jacks could be a bit of a challenge. Because of this, people had to get resourceful and cannibalize their jack collection with a "taw." While that may sound a bit extreme, it's actually quite simple since picking a taw is just a cool way of describing a jack that's picked out of the rest. To pick out said special jack, players use a process called "jockeying."

Though it sounds horse-related, jockeying is much simpler and doesn't require any short equestrians in weird pants. To jockey, a player would take a handful of jacks in one hand, toss them up, flip his hand, and try to catch as many as he can on the back of his hand. The player would then toss up those caught jacks and again flip his hand, trying to catch the remaining jacks in his palm. This process keeps repeating until there's one lucky jack left in the player's hand—and that becomes his taw!

OTHER WAYS TO PLAY

The Flying Dutchman

In this airborne variation, players must toss the ball into the air, scoop up the jacks, and catch the ball before it bounces all with one hand! In order to pass the jacks from the throwing hand to the holding hand, players are allowed to bounce the ball once and only once. If you've got good juggling skills, this is the game for you.

Eggs in a Basket

This popular variation of Jacks takes the original rules and somehow manages to make the game even more challenging! In Eggs in a Basket, the player takes his turn as he would in a standard game of Jacks. The difference, however, is that now the player must put his other hand (the one not bouncing the ball and scooping jacks) on the ground, palm facing up and curled into a cup. While collecting the jacks, the player is now required to drop all collected jacks into the cupped hand (or basket) before catching the ball. Missing the basket and dropping jacks to the floor instead counts as a foul and will end the turn.

Through the Arch

The "arch" in this game is made with the player's thumb and index finger. Put the tips of the index finger and thumb of your other hand on the ground, to make a wide arch. The player then tosses up the ball and attempts to sweep a single jack under the arch before catching the ball. Once all the jacks have made their way through the arch, the player closes the deal by tossing the ball up one last time and going for all the jacks at once in one big sweep.

Sequences

Possibly the hardest variation of them all, sequences starts off easy as any regular game of Jacks, with the player throwing the ball in the air and attempting onesies on the first try. However, on the next try he must do twosies, then threesies, then foursies, all while keeping the jacks in one hand the entire time! Upon making foursies, the player will have all ten jacks in her hand. The next and most challenging step is to bounce the ball once and drop all the jacks, only to attempt tensies immediately afterward! Because of the level of difficulty, only a few proud players can lay claim to being a sequences master.

Jacks' Terms

Do you think *knucklebones*, *taw*, and *jockey* sound odd? Try rolling some of these other Jacks' terms off of your tongue.

SWEEPS

This is the act of brushing the jacks along the floor with your fingers. Sweeping is often used to get fallen jacks out of the way or, in some cases, to play a variation game.

TIPPING

Tipping occurs when you accidentally move a jack when you're not supposed to do so, usually when you're trying to grab one jack and hit or tip another.

SCATTERS

As the name implies, scattering is the act of spreading the jacks on the floor, usually to begin a new game.

DUMPS

Not all games of Jacks require scattering—some require dumps. Dumping is when you unload the jacks into a small pile.

NO DUMPS

Because scatters and dumps can lead to two different types of game play, players often make known their preference by calling "No dumps," meaning players have to scatter the jacks instead of dumping them.

BREAKS

Did you dump the jacks when you were supposed to scatter them? Solve the problem by pulling breaks—the act of hitting a dumped pile of jacks to scatter them across the floor.

TIC TAC TOE
The Ultimate Fight for Territory!

Game Stats

STYLE: Strategy Game
PLAYERS: Two
REQUIREMENTS:
Writing implement
Paper
SKILLS:
Strategic thinking
Patience
Excellent grid
   drawing abilities

- - - - - - - - - - -

ALSO KNOWN AS
X-O
Xies
Osies
Naughts and Crosses
Xs and Os

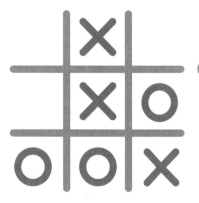

WHAT IT IS

A true classic, Tic Tac Toe has earned its place as a go-to recess game. It's easy to see why: it's quick (some games last less than a minute), it's easy to learn (there's really only one rule), and you can play it anywhere (at a desk with a pen and paper or on the recess yard with chalk on blacktop). Despite its simplicity, few games challenge the mind like Tic Tac Toe does.

WHAT'S THE POINT?

Players take turns marking up sections of the grid with their own letter. The first person to mark three grids in a row—horizontally, vertically, or diagonally—is the winner.

HOW YOU PLAY

1 Hash it out

The game starts with a player drawing a large 3 × 3 grid, which looks exactly like a hashtag (also known as a "pound" or "number sign"). Both players decide on who is "X" and who is "O," then they decide who goes first. If this is not easily determined, check out our section on Firsts on page 14.

2 Make your mark

The first player picks one of the nine boxes created in by the grid and labels it with his mark, with the ultimate goal of lining up three marks in a row horizontally, vertically, or diagonally.

3 Make your move or block the shot

The second player then puts her mark on to the grid. She can either attempt to connect her own row of three marks, or prevent the other player from doing so by blocking off one of the grids, forcing him to try to find another way to connect three in a row.

EXPERT STRATEGIES
If Possible, Go First
Statistically speaking, the first player has a better chance of winning. When looking at the likelihood of a win, the first player has 131,184 possible winning outcomes, while the player who goes second only has 77,904 possible winning outcomes. (In case you're curious, there are 46,080 outcomes that would lead to a draw.)

Corners Rule
If you're going first, always start with a corner. As long as your opponent doesn't pick the center square, you'll have a fairly good likelihood of winning.

Don't Fall for the Middle Spot
Never pick the middle spot first. Doing so has the most probability of the game ending in a tie.

Unless You're Up Second
If you're going second, always pick the middle square. Doing so likely won't end with a win, but at the very least it will cause a draw.

OTHER WAYS TO PLAY
Qubic
This version of Tic Tac Toe is played on a 4 × 4 × 4 grid, upping the amount of possible winning outcomes and lowering the likelihood of a draw.

Straight 15
This version—invented by mathematician R. Graham—replaces Xs and Os with the numbers one to nine. One player assumes the odd numbers while the other takes the evens. Each player takes turns putting one number down in the grid (they can only use each number once) with the goal of being the first to connect three squares with three numbers that equal exactly fifteen.

Coach Says . . .

No one wants to hear this, but the better the players, the more likely every game ends in a dreaded tie.

COOTIE CATCHER
The Future . . . in the Palm of Your Hand!

Game Stats

STYLE: Prediction game

PLAYERS: Two (one person to operate the Cootie Catcher, and another to ask the questions)

REQUIREMENTS:

A piece of paper

Scissors

Markers or crayons, pencil or pen

SKILLS:

Agile fingers

A basic understanding of origami (paper folding)

The ability to accept your fate, no matter what it may hold

- - - - - - - - - - -

ALSO KNOWN AS

Paper Fortune-teller

Paper Trap

Chatterbox

Salt Cellar

Whirlybird

WHAT IT IS

What if you could see into the future? What if you knew who you would marry, or what you would do when you grew up? That would be amazing—right? Unfortunately, only time will be able to truly answer those questions for you. But for those of us who are a little less patient, and a little more optimistic, there's the Cootie Catcher, a fortune-teller that adds fun to the guessing game known as life.

WHAT'S THE POINT?

Players ask the fortune-teller (a.k.a. the person operating the Cootie Catcher) a question. Then, using a series of numbers and colors, the Cootie Catcher answers that question and reveals the player's destiny.

HOW YOU PLAY

1 Create your destiny

Taking a simple piece of loose-leaf paper, the fortune-teller folds and cuts the sheet to create the amazing Cootie Catcher (detailed instructions on the next spread).

2 Question fate

With the Cootie Catcher complete, the fortune-teller begins taking questions from the other players, one at a time. Players can ask the fortune-teller any question, as long as it can be answered with "yes," "no," or "maybe."

3 Count on chance

Once the player asks a question, the fortune-teller must request a number from the player. Depending on the player's answer, the fortune-teller then opens and closes the Cootie Catcher with their thumbs and index fingers many times.

4 Color your future

This should now leave the Cootie Catcher open and revealing four colors. The player picks one color, and the fortune-teller lifts up the flap of that color, answering the player's question and giving them a brief glimpse into what fortune awaits them!

Approved Cootie Catcher Fortunes

Predicting a future is serious business. What you write can literally change someone's life. OK, not life, but day. OK, not day, but mood. So here are several prime fortune ideas. Please use wisely.

As sure as the sun burns.	Don't look behind you.
Only the stars truly know.	Something you lost will soon turn up.
You will have very good luck today.	You will get an "A" on that test.
A secret admirer will soon show how they feel.	You will be rich.
The more you give, the more you'll have.	Good fortune will be yours.
Don't give up.	Someone will call you today.
The one you love is closer than you think.	You will go to a party soon.
It's time to make new friends.	Be careful on Tuesday.
Don't know, ask the fortune cookie.	Good luck is coming your way.
A scented eraser is in your future.	Watch what you step in.
Bad times are ahead.	

Creating a Cootie Catcher

As a beginning fortune-teller, one of the most important skills you can learn is how to create your own Cootie Catcher. While reading minds and speaking to the dead are great skills, turning a simple piece of paper into a Cootie Catcher is a craft and an art form that, when done right, will separate you from all the wannabe palm readers out there!

To begin, you'll need a regular sheet of 8½ x 11 paper, scissors, a pen, and some markers or crayons. After that, follow these simple steps:

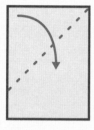

1 Fold the top corner down and over so it meets the opposite side.

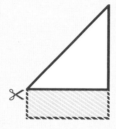

2 Cut the paper that's left underneath along the bottom edge of the triangle.

3 When you unfold the sheet, it should now be a square.

4 Fold the other corner of the paper up and over towards the opposite side.

5 When it's done, unfold and you'll have an "X" creased across the flat sheet.

6 Take the four corners and fold them into the center.

7 With these corners folded inward, flip the paper over.

8 Fold the four corners inward a second time so that all four corners are folded to meet in the middle.

9 Once the Cootie Catcher is folded properly, write the numbers on the outside as shown and then lift each flap and write answers on the inside. Answers like "Yes," "No," "Maybe," and "Ask Again" are fine, but more creative things are better—see the list on the previous spread.

FOLD IT IN HALF

TURN IT UPSIDE DOWN

10 Fold the flaps back in and flip the Cootie Catcher over and color each panel a different color or your choice. Have fun with the designs and shapes if you want to get custom!

11 Finally, fold the Cootie Catcher in half again.

12 Turn it around and wiggle your thumbs and index fingers into the open slots and let the fun begin!

3 THIRD PERIOD
JUMPING & ROPE GAMES

Flights of Fancy Taken Daily

What a happy talent to know how to play.
— **Ralph Waldo Emerson**

There is a reason people having a wild time are described as "bouncing off the wall." It's because bouncing is just fun. Whether it's on the squares of the hopscotch court or around a swinging jump rope—jumping games are the perfect combination of stamina, skill, and most interestingly, rhythm. This chapter also includes Tug of War, which might not directly involve jumping—but if played with enough vigor, people could take flight.

A Classic Game That Is the Chalk of the Town

Game Stats

STYLE: Jumping game

PLAYERS: One or more

REQUIREMENTS:

A flat, hard surface

A drawn court (either
  prepainted or drawn with
  chalk)

Something to use as a
  marker (e.g., rock,
  bottle cap)

SKILLS:

Balance

Nimbleness

Hoppability

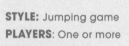

FUN FACT

The game dates back to at
least the early 1600s—where
recess game researchers
have found references to
"Scotch Hoppers"—mean-
ing jumping over a line or
scotch.

WHAT IT IS

There are few games that capture the innocence of child-
hood as much as Hopscotch. And there are few games as
widely played. Cultures from around the world have their
own versions of the simple hopping and balancing game.
In the pantheon of games, Hopscotch doesn't immediately
appear remarkable. It's relatively slow, doesn't boast any
catchy songs or difficult aerial maneuvers. But what makes it
so unremarkable is also what makes it so approachable and
beloved.

WHAT'S THE POINT?

While different versions are played the world over, the general idea is that a player must hop over lines while keeping
balanced. The most common rule variation lies in the order
in which the squares must be jumped. The first player to
complete the series wins. But, in general, it's less about
beating your opponents and more about having more time
on the grid.

HOW YOU PLAY

1 Choose your court

On some playgrounds, the court is painted directly on the
surface. If yours doesn't have one, don't worry. A court can
be drawn on to the ground with a piece of chalk.

As you'll see from the illustration, there are varieties of for-
mations, but the basic Western court design is a grid measuring about 10 feet long and numbered 1 to 10. The last square
can have a number or word like "safe," "home," "rest," or
"out." The general rule is that you can only step with one
foot in any of the squares. If two squares are side by side, you
can step with one foot in each square—and at that point, you
can switch feet for the next hop.

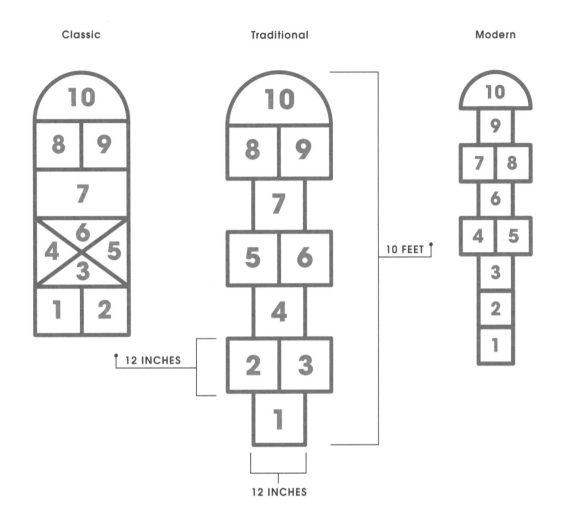

Classic   Traditional   Modern

12 INCHES

10 FEET

12 INCHES

Coach Says . . .

Which foot you hop with is up to you. I recommend choosing the foot you most commonly hop on. But, hey, that's just me.

② **Choose your marker**

Any flat easy-to-throw object can be used as a marker. The ideal marker can tossed with suitable accuracy, but most importantly, it won't roll or bounce away. It should be easy to pick up and small enough that it can fit in your pocket when it's time to head back inside.

HOPSCOTCH MARKERS 101

An often overlooked and underappreciated part of Hopscotch is the marker—also known as the shooter or taw. The right marker can make all the difference between getting the right throw or having it roll out of bounds—and down the drain.

In the early- to mid-1900s, New Yorkers called the game Potsie, or Potsy, in reference to the marker, which was held in high regard. Kids would look far and wide to find the best object and would have serious bragging rights. Potsies were traded, sold, stolen, and cherished. Making markers more important again is part of keeping Hopscotch "topscotch."

Time to continue that tradition into today. Below are several classic solutions:

OLD SHOE HEEL—In the age of sneakers, it's harder to find but the heavy rubber of an old men's formal shoe has heft, softness, and little "roll-ability."

BEANBAG—A beanbag left over from a throwing game or an old beloved and very broken in beanie animal—it's a classic choice that you won't go wrong with.

OLD HOCKEY PUCK—If you can get your hands on one that is not being used in someone else's game, then toss away.

SMALL PLASTIC TOY—Provide a second life for an old toy. Choose one that is from heavier plastic without any articulated parts. Just a colorful chunk of marker awesomeness.

HOPPY TAW—This manufactured rubber puck is make specifically for Hopscotch. It often comes in a variety of lively colors—making it highly collectable and tradable.

❸ Throw that starts the show

The player with Firsts starts by throwing her marker into box no. 1. It must land completely in the box—without touching any of the lines. Then, she begins to hop through all of the boxes to the end of the court—but always avoiding the box with the marker in it. On the way back, she must stop and pick up the marker before hopping out through the end of the grid.

❹ Taking (or not taking) turns

If the player is able to complete her turn without committing a foul, she maintains control and gets to throw her marker into box no. 2 and repeat the process. If she commits a foul, she will have to wait to pick up her turn after the other players have their hops at the court.

❺ Losing a turn

The goal of a game is keeping your turn, but if you commit any of these fouls, you must forfeit your turn:

- Failure to throw the marker fully inside the intended box
- Throwing the marker in the wrong box
- Stepping on any of the box lines
- Stepping into the box with the marker
- Using your hands to support yourself when picking up the marker
- Using two feet in one square
- Falling down

❻ Winning the game

The first player to complete the whole series (from the first to last box, including "out" or "rest" if it's not numbered) wins the game and gets to hop for joy. But in most cases, the victory is less important than getting more time on the grid to hop around.

FUN FACT

Homolateral movement is the technical term for moving one side of the body while keeping the other side still, like hopping on one foot. And it's one of the most complex movements the human body can perform.

THROWING TECHNIQUES

Hopping gets all the attention in Hopscotch—and rightfully so. But the accuracy of a throw is what really gets the game moving.

Underhanded

This is not about your strategy but your throwing style. You'll want to be as gentle and accurate as possible. Power has no place here, so use a soft underhanded throw to place the marker in the right location.

No Spin Zone

As tempting as it is to throw the marker like a Frisbee, don't do it. Spinning might help objects go farther distances—but you'll pay the price when it rolls out of bounds.

Aim Low

Grand dreams of winning start down low on the ground. Knowing that the momentum will carry the marker past its initial landing point, aiming right beneath the number works well for some people.

Coach Says . . .

Just because your nonhopping leg is not touching the ground, doesn't mean it's not part of the action. Use your other leg to help propel with a subtle backward air kick.

OTHER WAYS TO PLAY

Hopscotch with Kicks

There are several versions of Hopscotch that involve kicking as a central element. In one variation, the player throws her marker, but once she reaches the marked box, she must kick her marker completely out of the grid. In another variation, the marker is not thrown into a box, it's kicked—like a soccer dribble—through each of the boxes.

3	4	9	10	13	16	19
2	5	8	11	14	17	20
1	6	7	12	15	18	21

Window Hopscotch

The court looks complicated but the game play is quite familiar. A large rectangle is divided into 21 numbered boxes. The first player throws her marker onto any box and hops on one foot through the sequential numbers to that location. If successful, she claims that square and can use it as a rest stop to use for both feet, while other players must jump over it.

Freestyle Hopscotching

There is a side to this classic game that has yet to be fully realized: customization. With just a piece of chalk, players can create their own court with any number of unique features. Boxes can be shaped and oriented in any direction. Some boxes can be "islands" and require a sizable jump to land on. Boxes can have instructions of actions to be performed when touched. Any way you play it, a unique grid offers a challenge for the players' hopping abilities and creativity.

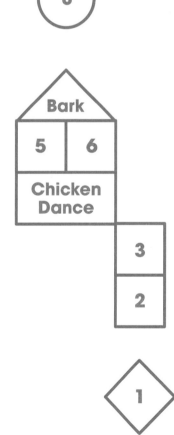

WORLD OF PLAY

Hopscotch is a game that has truly, um, hopped around the world. Grab your chalk and passport and check out the following worldly variations:

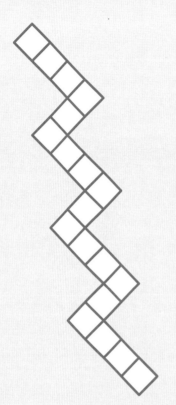

JAPANESE HOPSCOTCH

This version is best played with two to three players. The court includes nineteen unnumbered one-foot squares in a snakelike pattern (see the following illustration). No marker is used, but a piece of chalk is required.

The game play is simple—yet full of strategy. The first player hops through the whole court on one foot. Once she reaches the other end, she picks any square to claim by writing her initial in the space. In subsequent turns, she can step with both feet in her square. But the other players cannot set foot in it—and they must jump over it. There are no back-to-back turns, so the game continues one player at a time—and with each successful trip through the court, more squares are claimed. The player who initials the most squares at the end of the game wins.

FRENCH HOPSCOTCH

The French version, also known as Escargot, is similar to the Japanese version—but with a French twist, of course. Rather than an angular shape, the French court resembles a snail's shell—a spiral with sections divided into numbered boxes. The game play mirrors the Japanese version with the prize for a successful trip being that the player can initial a box to claim it. Again, they can now step with both feet, but the other players can't step in that box at all.

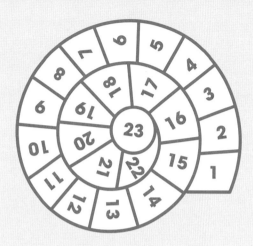

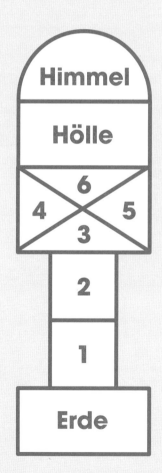

HIMMEL UND HÖLLE

The game is frequently called Himmel und Hölle (Heaven and Hell) in Germany, Austria, and Switzerland. Below box no. 1 is a box called Erde (Earth), while the second to last box is the Hölle (Hell), and the last one is Himmel (Heaven). The first player throws a small stone into the first box and then jumps to that box. Then he kicks the stone to the next one before hopping forward. The "Hell" location is where neither the stone nor the player can stop so everyone must hop over it to get to "Heaven."

Here are some of the names of other Hopscotch games from around the world:

- Bebeleche (Mexico)
- Campana (Italy)
- Ekaria Dukaria (India)
- Hinkelbaan (Netherlands)
- Klasy (Poland)
- La Peregrina (Puerto Rico)
- Pico (Vietnam)
- Rayuela (Argentina)
- Seksek (Turkey)

JUMP ROPE
Swing Rope, Jump over Rope, Repeat

Game Stats

STYLE: Jumping game
PLAYERS: One
REQUIREMENTS:
A jump rope (basically a
   rope with handles)
SKILLS:
Good hand-eye
   coordination
Fast feet
Patience

WHAT IT IS
Jump rope is the ultimate self-imposed challenge of one's physicality. What at first seems like a simple task of jumping in place can quickly become an marathon-like challenge that tests both dexterity and stamina, all while forcing you to keep count of how many times you were able to jump without stumbling. And all this is before you even begin to incorporate trick jumps and maneuvers. Because of this and the dominance it claimed during the more primal days of recess, Jump Rope will always have a place high up on the pedestal of classic playground activities.

WHAT'S THE POINT?
Jumping rope, as the name implies, revolves around jumping over a rope. The point is to jump over the rope as many times consecutively as possible without stumbling. This can be done by straight up jumping, or it can be done with little touches of flare, depending on the jumper's preference.

HOW YOU PLAY
1 Rope it in
Begin by finding a good jump rope. While there are ropes specifically made for jumping rope, you can get by with just any piece of rope. For best results, make sure the rope has some weight to it (the lighter the rope, the more difficult it will be for beginners).

2 Ankle up
Start by holding one end of the rope in each hand, with your elbows tucked in at your sides and your hands at about waist height. The middle portion of the rope should be touching the backs of your ankles.

3 Hop, skip, and a jump
When starting, swing the rope over your head. As the rope comes down toward the ground, hop over it. Keep the rope swinging in that motion and repeat each time it approaches your feet. And that's it!

Coach Says . . .

How do you know if the jump rope you have is right for you? If you're a beginner, simply take the rope and put your foot on the middle of it. The top of the handles should come up to right around your shoulders. If you've done this a bit before, then the handles should come up to about your armpits.

OTHER WAYS TO PLAY

You thought it was as simple as just jumping over a rope? Well, you were right, but you can also add these variations to put some bump in your jump.

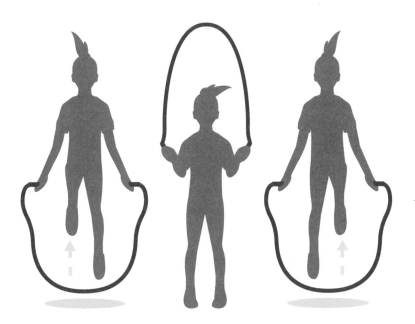

The Back and Forth

On each jump, use only one foot, keeping the other foot a little higher. On the next jump, switch feet so the other foot is jumping. Go back and forth to add a little extra rhythm to your routine.

Double Under

Is the standard technique a little slow for your taste? Try pulling off a double under, which requires swinging the rope so fast that you're able to get it under your feet twice on a single jump.

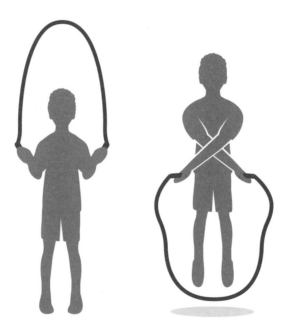

The Crisscross

This is just like your standard jump rope technique, but your hands cross over to the other side of the body, giving the rope and extra crossing motion to ramp up difficulty.

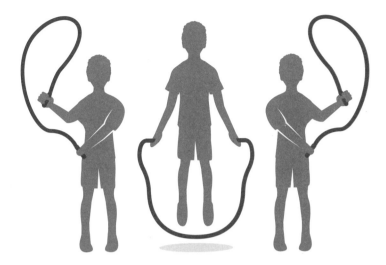

Side Swing Take your Crisscross to the next level by throwing in a side-swing. This move doesn't involve jumping over the rope, but actually swinging it to the side between jumps.

Front-Back Cross
Just like the Crisscross, only instead of crossing both hands in front of him, the jumper crosses one hand in front of him and one behind him, causing the rope to travel in a more "sideways" direction before righting itself in time for the next jump.

Toad

Ready for a challenge? To pull this off, the jumper performs the Crisscross-like move while one arm crosses over the body and below the opposite leg. Think it sounds complicated? Try doing it.

Double Up

If you're ready to take the next leap, but aren't quite ready to go it alone with the fancy tricks, try bringing in a partner—preferably one you don't mind sharing some personal space with. Get a slightly longer rope and stand facing your friend so you're almost, but not quite, nose-to-nose. Begin jumping rope as usual with one person holding the rope. It may take some time to get into the rhythm, but once you're in sync, it's magic!

Jump Rope Tips for Beginners

Whether you're playing Double Dutch or skipping solo, jumping rope can be a difficult skill to learn for beginners. Here are a few tips to help you jump in feet first.

GO ROPELESS

The best way to get used to jumping rope is to do it without an actual rope. Take this time to practice your form and get your movements and rhythm down.

START SLOW

Nobody expects you to do double under on your first try. In fact, *Muscle & Fitness* magazine suggests moving as slow as possible and possibly using a heavier rope until you start to develop the appropriate rhythm.

MASTER FORM AND FUNCTION

Make sure to focus more on your form than your feet—thinking too much about your jumping may throw off your timing. More importantly, focus on your pace. It's easy to get into the habit of "double jumping"—adding an extra jump after jumping over the rope—but this will only prevent you from improving your speed and technique going forward. Be sure to jump *only* when the rope hits the ground.

REFLECT

One should reflect—literally, in a mirror. If you have a reflective surface (a mirror or window) handy, watch yourself while you're jumping. This will help you keep a proper form and forget about your feet long enough to let them jump on their own.

PICK UP THE PACE

Once you clear the rope ten times without stumbling, increase the speed a little more and repeat, trying to clear ten jumps at a faster pace. Repeat this process until you're jumping at full speed without even counting.

DOUBLE DUTCH
Several People Jump, But Everybody Plays

Game Stats

STYLE: Jumping game
PLAYERS: Three or more
REQUIREMENTS:
Two jump ropes about 12 to
    14 feet long
A flat wide-open space
SKILLS:
Good hand-eye
    coordination
Fast feet
Spatial awareness
Patience

- - - - - - - - - - - -

ALSO KNOWN AS
Doubles Jump

WHAT IT IS
While its name sounds like it's from the most Dutch area of the Netherlands, it's a very American invention—courtesy of the playgrounds of New York City. Double Dutch's game play goes hand-in-hand with any other well-populated area since it's a game that's not only played by several people (the three or more jumping rope) but can also be enjoyed by spectators and waiting players who can passively participate by singing along with the rhymes that are usually chanted during each game.

WHAT'S THE POINT?
Double Dutch is often played in a competitive capacity, though it doesn't have to be. Each jumper (or team, if you're playing that way) attempts to jump as many times as possible without tripping on the rope. But it's also played more informally with individual players jumping in and taking turns.

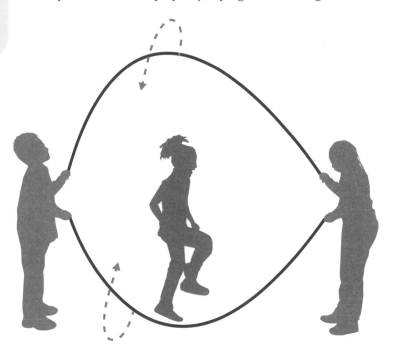

HOW YOU PLAY

1 Rope up

Two players, called the turners, each take the end of the ropes in each hand and face each other. They should be standing far enough apart for the ropes to hang slack enough so that they're just barely hovering above the ground.

2 Turn it up

Each turner will begin spinning the ropes by the handle. The players' left hands should be spinning the rope in a counter-clockwise motion while right hands should be spinning it in a clockwise motion. When one rope is at its highest point, the other rope should be at the point lowest to the ground. If that sounds like it can get a little difficult, it's because it can, but it's still not as difficult as the next part.

Coach Says . . .

Tip for turners: Imagine you're facing a wall and you want to keep the handles of the ropes touching the wall the whole time—this creates a more consistent turn for the jumpers.

Tip for jumpers: When starting off, it's easier to enter from an end closer to one of the turners. Instead of jumping in from the center at a right angle to the ropes, you'll be coming in at a 45-degree angle and have better vision of the ropes.

3 Jumping in

When she's ready, the third player (the jumper) watches the timing of the ropes and jumps in, one foot first. It's now up to her to keep jumping over each rope as it swoops below her. Once she stumbles or gets hit by a rope, it's the next player's turn.

4 Double up Double Dutch

If you have enough players, invite additional jumpers into the center. As long as the ropes are long enough, you can have several people jumping rope at once!

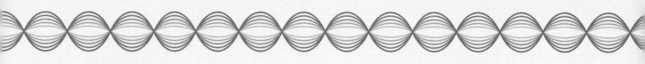

Jumping Rhymes

Both single rope jumping and Double Dutch have a long tradition of combining rhymes with the rhythm of the rope action. It's not only for keeping the tempo, it's also to help keep track of how long the jumper can keep on going.

As with all rhymes, half the fun is coming up with them on your own while playing. In the meantime, here are a couple classics to get you started.

BIRDIE BIRDIE:

Birdie, birdie in the sky,
Why'd ya do that in my eye?
Birdie, birdie in the sky,
Gee, I'm glad that cows don't fly.

TINY TIM:

I had a little puppy.
His name was Tiny Tim.
I put him in the bathtub,
To see if he could swim.
He drank up all the water.
He ate a bar of soap.
The next thing you know,
He had a bubble in his throat.
In came the doctor.
In came the nurse.
In came the lady.
With the alligator purse.
Out went the doctor. Out went the nurse.
Out went the lady.
With the alligator purse.

STRAWBERRY SWEETHEART:

Strawberry shortcake, cream on top
Tell me the name of your sweetheart:
A, B, C, D, E, F, G, H, I, J, etc.

(The letter shouted when the jumper misses is said to be the first letter of her sweetheart's name.)

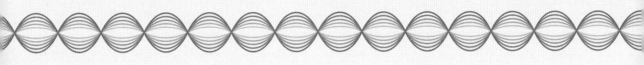

CALL THE ARMY:

Call the Army, call the Navy
So-so's gonna have a baby.
Wrap it up in tissue paper,
Send it down the elevator,
Boy, girl, twins, triplets, boys, girls, twins, triplets, etc.

(The word shouted when the jumper misses is the alleged
number of babies so-so's totally going to have.)

PEPPER:

Mabel, Mabel,
Set the table,
Don't forget the salt,
Vinegar, mustard, pepper! Vinegar, mustard, pepper!
etc.

(Every time the word "pepper" is said, the speed of the
rope spinning increases.)

CHARLIE CHAPLAN:

Charlie Chaplan went to France,
To teach the ladies how to dance,
First he did the Rumba,
Then he did the twist,
Then he did the Highland Fling,
And then he did the splits.

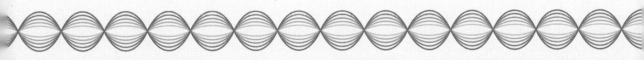

CHINESE JUMP ROPE
A Game of Precision, Rhythm, and Stretchiness

Game Stats

STYLE: Jumping and rhythm

PLAYERS: Ideally three (as few as one and as many as five)

REQUIREMENTS:

A large loop stretchy rope

Two things to hold it (if you don't have enough people)

SKILLS:

Mastery of jumping

Balance and dexterity

Memory

Foot-eye coordination

- - - - - - - - - -

ALSO KNOWN AS

Chinese Garters

Chinese Skip Rope

Elastics

French Skipping

Gummitwist

Jump Band

Jumpsies

Yogi

WHAT IT IS

Combine the hopping of Hopscotch with the twists of Cat's Cradle with a splash of tap dancing. The resulting concoction: Chinese Jump Rope. It offers a moderate amount of physical challenge, and the difficulty can be adjusted for every skill level, from novices to Olympians. While there are regional variations and traditions, it speaks the universal language: the language of jumping over a piece of rope. All of this and it requires one piece of equipment that you don't even need to buy. That, folks, is how to become a master of play.

WHAT'S THE POINT?

The point is to execute a series of difficult-to-replicate moves that get more difficult as the game progresses. If you nail it, you keep going. If you flub it, you step out of the jumping position and give someone else a turn. There is no real score to record or points to capture. It's just free flowing—or in this case, free jumping.

HOW YOU PLAY

1 Begin with the enders

Two people acting as the holders, also known as enders, stand several feet apart. An elastic rope wraps around their ankles and is taut enough that it doesn't touch the ground. The basic formation for the rope is a rectangle.

Coach Says . . .

If you don't have two people to serve as enders, you can simply use two chairs to hold the rope in position. Plus, you'll have a place to catch your break after nailing all the moves.

② Jumping jumper

The star of the show is the jumper who stands between the two enders. They must now execute a pattern of steps. Some people play very sophisticated variations with dance-like moves, but we like to start at the beginning. Some of the basic moves follow:

- **In:** This is when both feet are in the center rope rectangle.
- **Out:** When both feet are outside neither side of the ropes.
- **On:** When both feet are placed on top of the ropes.
- **Straddle:** This is when one foot is inside the frame and one is outside.
- **Diamonds:** Standing on one side, your near foot lifts the near side of the rope, pulls it up and over to create a diamond-shaped space to step into.
- **Twirlies:** Also known as twists; starting from the out position, you rotate 180 degrees, twisting the rope with your feet.

In a following section, we'll show how these moves are put into patterns with accompanying chants to create the routines of the games.

③ Raise the rope

Chinese Jump Rope adds new levels to the standard game—literally. Each time a jumper completes a routine without any faults, the enders raise the rope and the difficulty level. While the exact levels vary, following is the most common progression:

LEVEL 1: ankles
LEVEL 2: calves
LEVEL 3: knees
LEVEL 4: thighs
LEVEL 5: hips

④ Switching it up

The first jumper continues to play and attempts higher and higher levels, until they commit a fault. At which point they switch with one of the enders and have to wait to return to the jumper position. The most common faults include: **(a)** missing part of the pattern, **(b)** touching the rope at the wrong time, and **(c)** falling down or touching the ground with one's hands.

FUN FACT

The game originated in seventh century China, and has been popular in the United States since the 1960s.

SAFETY PATROL: Playing on grass lowers the risk of scrapes or pavement "burns," especially when the rope is raised to higher levels.

JUMPING PATTERNS

Jumping patterns vary greatly and can be created on the spot with your friends. Following are four versions of the more common ones to get you started.

BASIC

1. Start with both feet on one side of the rope
2. Jump in with both feet, say "in"
3. Jump out with both feet, say "out"
4. Straddle left elastic, say "side"
5. Straddle right elastic, say "side"
6. Jump in with both feet, say "in"
7. Jump out with both feet, say "out"
8. Jump on ropes, say "on"

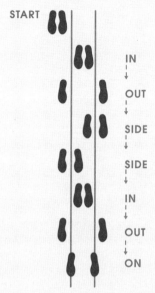

START

IN
↓
OUT
↓
SIDE
↓
SIDE
↓
IN
↓
OUT
↓
ON

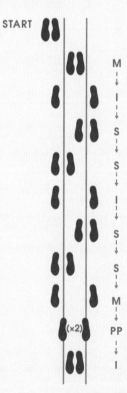

START

M
↓
I
↓
I
↓
S
↓
S
↓
I
↓
S
↓
S
↓
M
↓
(×2) PP
↓
I

MISSISSIPPI

1. Start with both feet on one side of the rope
2. Jump in with both feet, say "m"
3. Jump out with both feet, say "i"
4. Straddle left elastic, say "s"
5. Straddle right elastic, say "s"
6. Jump out with both feet, say "i"
7. Straddle left elastic, say "s"
8. Straddle right elastic, say "s"
9. Jump out with both feet, say "i"
10. Double jump on ropes, say "pp"
11. Jump out with both feet, say "i"

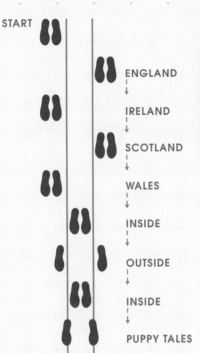

START

ENGLAND

IRELAND

SCOTLAND

WALES

INSIDE

OUTSIDE

INSIDE

PUPPY TALES

ENGLAND, IRELAND

1. Start with both feet on one side of the rope
2. Jump over with both feet, say "England"
3. Jump back over with both feet, say "Ireland"
4. Jump over with both feet, say "Scotland"
5. Jump back over with both feet, say "Wales"
6. Jump so both feet land on the inside, say "inside"
7. Jump so both feet land on each outside, say "outside"
8. Jump so both feet land on the inside, say "inside"
9. Land on both ropes, say "puppy tails"

This rhyme also ends with "monkey tails," "kitten tails," and "donkey tails" depending on where you grew up.

EXPERT LEVEL

1. Start with both feet on one side of the rope
2. Jump in with both feet, say "in"
3. Jump out with both feet, say "out"
4. Step on ropes, say "on"
5. Jump in with both feet, say "in"
6. Jump out with both feet, say "out"
7. Twist 180 degrees to the left, say "twist"
8. Jump out of the twisted ropes, say "out"
9. Twist 180 degrees to right, say "twist"
10. Jump out of the twisted ropes, say "out"
11. Step in from the left side to make a diamond, say "diamond"
12. Jump out of the twisted ropes, say "out"
13. Step in from the right side to make a diamond, say "diamond"
14. Jump out of the twisted ropes, say "out"

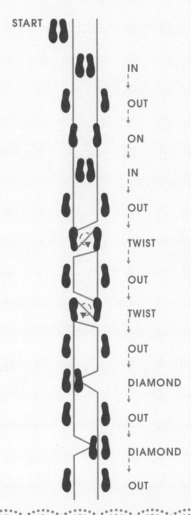

START

IN

OUT

ON

IN

OUT

TWIST

OUT

TWIST

OUT

DIAMOND

OUT

DIAMOND

OUT

WORLD OF PLAY

Chinese Jump Rope is played all over the world. In German-speaking countries, children call it "Gummites." In Great Britain and New Zealand it's called Elastics, in Canada it is Jumpsies or Yoki, and in the Kaiser and Estonia, it is Kummikeks.

CHINESE JUMP ROPES 101

- **THE PURCHASED ROPE**
  10 to 12 feet long
  Joined ends
- **THE DIY ROPE**
  ⅜ inch braided elastic from fabric store
  Safety pins to fasten
- **THE REALLY DIY ROPE**
  Approximately 40 rubber bands
  Interlocking chain

OPTIONAL RULES

- Designate "no touching" levels, which a player must "clear" when jumping.

- Player forfeits a turn if the rope is touched at these levels.

- Allow player to use her hand to lower the elastic when jumping at a high level.

- Some versions allow the jumper to do the pattern with their hands if the rope is over the armpits.

OTHER WAYS TO PLAY

Skinnies
Skinnies is when each ender puts her feet together, instead of shoulder-width apart, to create a smaller, more difficult space, for the jumper to enter.

Fats
Fats is the opposite of skinnies, each ender spreads her feet apart to create a larger space—which in turn, creates a larger area for the jumper to jump across. This is also known as wides.

Ice Cream Cones
Ice cream cones is when one ender holds the rope with one foot on one end while the other uses two feet to create a triangle, or cone shape.

Scissors
This is when the enders synchronize the movement of their feet—shuffling them in and out, creating a moving parallelogram out of the traditional rectangular rope shape.

TUG OF WAR
A Struggle Between Two Forces—And Rope Burn

WHAT IT IS

Tug of War is quite literally a struggle between two forces. Add to that a range of risk that goes from pesky clothing stains to possible dismemberment (more on avoiding that later), and you have the makings of quite possibly the most epic game in history. Who started this war of tugging is unknown, but there is evidence it has been played in ancient Egypt, Greece, and China. Today, it's standard on playgrounds and at picnics, family reunions, company outings, and not surprisingly, Tug of War competitions.

WHAT'S THE POINT?

The goal is to win the war of the tug. The two sides pull in opposites directions trying to get the rope to move more on to their side. The game is over when one team overpowers the other. Most matches are played best of three.

Game Stats

STYLE: Test of strength

PLAYERS: Four to eighteen (two evenly matched teams)

REQUIREMENTS:

One large rope

Tape

A marker (to mark the center starting line on the ground)

SKILLS:

Grip strength

Back strength

Leg strength

Detergent strength (for grass stains)

- - - - - - - - - - -

ALSO KNOWN AS

Rope Pulling

Rope War

Tug o' War

Tug War

Tugging War

HOW YOU PLAY

1 Readying the rope

The rope is marked with a center line and two markings 4 yards on either side of the center line. If playing with kids, the markings can be moved to 2 yards on either side. A marker of some sort (e.g., a cone, a rock, a stick) should be placed in the ground as well.

SAFETY PATROL

A quick search into the dangers of Tug of War will result in some disturbing results. We don't want to get into the details, but let's just say it isn't pretty. But like many games, a few safety precautions can go a long way.

ONE TRUE ROPE

Only use rope that is made of natural manila—it'll absorb sweat so it doesn't get slippery and, most importantly, it doesn't stretch and recoil like nylon does.

NO LOOPING

Never wrap the rope around your hands or arms. This places you at risk for bad stuff happening, like dislocations and other uncomfortable and unfortunate injuries.

NATURAL GRIP ONLY

The safest way to hold the rope is with both palms facing up with fingers wrapped around the rope.

SAFE ANCHORING

The anchor is at most risk for injury if the rope breaks. The recommended form is that the rope passes alongside the body, diagonally across the back, and over the opposite shoulder from rear to front. Any extra rope goes under the armpit and out the back—staying away from any tripping risks.

② Selecting and setting teams

Two captains choose and organize their teams. While each captain is looking for a competitive advantage, the game is usually the most entertaining when teams are equally matched in size and strength. There are only two positions in Tug of War. The anchors who control the ends of the rope are often the largest and strongest members of each team. The pullers are, well, everyone else.

③ Pulling with purpose

At the starting signal, the teams pull with all their might. Each team attempts to move the rope in their direction. The first team to get the outside marking on the other side of the rope to cross the center marker wins. The other way to win is if the other team commits a foul.

④ Fouls aplenty

While not often enforced during informal matches, serious Tug of War players need to respect a short list of rules that ensure the game is both competitive and safe. A foul is committed if: **(a)** any team member sits or falls down on the ground, **(b)** any team member steps or falls into the neutral zone, or **(c)** any team suddenly lets go of the rope and deliberately causes the opposing team to fall over.

PULLING TECHNIQUES

A proper pulling position isn't just hard to pronounce—it's hard to do without a little bit of preparation. The following steps should provide some good technique foundation: **(a)** hold the rope at waist level through your center of gravity, **(b)** stand at a 45 degree angle keeping your back straight, and **(c)** take short steps, using the strength of your legs to move your body.

Coach Says . . .

Flip-flops have no role in Tug of War. The more solid the footwear, the better advantage you have. Shoes are good and boots are the best.

WORLD OF PLAY

Tug of War could be Tug of War of the Worlds because it is played all across the globe. Here are some different traditions of this beloved game:

AFGHANISTAN: A wooden stake is used instead of a rope.

KOREA: A giant version called juldarigi uses two huge rice-straw ropes

BASQUE COUNTRY: Tug of War is an important part of their traditional rural games—in Spanish this is called *sogatira* and in French *tir à la corde.*

EXPERT STRATEGIES

Tug of War is more than just the tug—it involves technique, too. There are two basic moves that when used along with brute force will get you closer to the sweet taste of victory.

Rhythm Method

This method is simply a coordinated group effort where, at the rhythm called out by one of the pullers, everyone yanks at the same time. If the competition is formidable, the result will not be a massive gain, but it can be effective in small incremental inches that over time will bring it home.

Rest Method

This is the yang to the yin of the rhythm method. When the competition is pulling, the best defense is for everyone on the team to dig into the ground with their feet in the lockdown position. This is held until the opponent tires, making pulling them over the marker that much easier.

OTHER WAYS TO PLAY:
TRIANGULAR TUG OF WAR

All the tugging, all the war, half the size. A 10-foot rope is tied into a loop and three players grab it with one hand each—gently pulling it taut and creating a triangle shape. An object (e.g., a flag, rock) is placed several feet away from each of the players. At the signal, each player must compete to reach the object without letting go of the rope.

THE PIT OF DESPAIR

This variation is played with the same traditional Tug of War rules, but with one exception: there's a swimming pool, small pond, or massive mud pit in the middle of the opposing teams' markers. A team wins not only by pulling the rope past their marker, but also by pulling the opposing team into the mud. As each member falls in, they are out of the contest.

STUMPS OF WAR

Also known simply as stumps, this version is perfect when you only have two players and lots of extra room. Each player stands on a tree stump (milk crates or cinder blocks also work) about 10 feet apart. They each hold the ends of a 30-foot rope that is coiled in the middle. The goal is simple: get as much rope as possible and pull your competitor off her stump.

FUN FACT

Tug of War was featured in the Olympic Games from 1900 to 1920. Countries that won gold medals are Sweden (2), Great Britain (2) and USA (1).

4

BALL GAMES

If It Rolls, Bounces, or Flies— It's Game Time.

The ball: one of the greatest discoveries in human history. We can only assume a fruit dropped between two Neanderthals who likely started to chuck it at each other's giant forehead. Playing games with rolling objects is just that natural. Ball games appear on the monuments of ancient Egypt, in the stories of ancient Greece, and in the backyards of homes around the world. Apparently, ball games are, in fact, how we roll. And bounce. And throw.

FOUR SQUARE
A Classic Battle over Four Quadrants, and a Famous Red Ball

Game Stats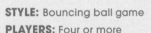

STYLE: Bouncing ball game

PLAYERS: Four or more

REQUIREMENTS:

Playground ball (preferably red)

Court

SKILLS:

Speed

Agility

Ball control

Strategy

- - - - - - - - - - -

ALSO KNOWN AS:

Blockball

Boxball

King's Corners

Squareball

WHAT IT IS

Four Square has become one of the most played and celebrated games on the blacktop for a multitude of reasons. For one, the game requires just a playground ball and a small patch of hard surface, so a match can be easily set up. The rules are simple to follow but provide plenty of room for a creative spin, so it's totally customizable, and the game play is approachable enough to attract a wide range of players. On top of that, the revolving door nature of the game mixes players up constantly, allowing for alliances to be rapidly made and broken, and keeps even those waiting in line to join the game on their toes.

WHAT'S THE POINT?

The game play is simple: four players each occupy a quarter of a small square court, bouncing a ball between them until someone makes an error and is eliminated. Eliminated players leave the court, all players advance to fill the empty squares, and a new player joins at the lowest ranked square.

While some people keep track of games won as points, the most common and preferred objective is simply to remain in the top position—the fourth square—in order to have more playing time, be able to make and revise rules, and enjoy the thrill of being the king.

HOW YOU PLAY
1 Set up the ground rules

As you'll see, there are numerous rules and variations of play that can make this game great. But this can lead to arguments if the baseline rules aren't established before the start of the game. The player serving can always call out additional rules for that particular round, but everyone needs the same starting point.

② Set up the court

Four Square is played on a 16 feet × 16 feet court divided into four smaller 8 feet × 8 feet squares that meet in the center. Squares are ranked from highest to lowest (four, three, two, one), with the fourth square being the best. You can also use letters (A, B, C, D—A is in the no. 4-spot), or even the title of royalty (King, Queen, Jack, Dunce—King is in the no. 1-spot). In all cases, the highest and lowest ranked squares should be diagonal from each other.

A small box, called the mailbox is often drawn in the far corner for the highest square to signify where the player should stand when serving.

Following are the two sets of lines on the court—outside lines making up the outermost edges of the entire court—and inside lines, which divide the individual squares: **(a)** Outside lines are in-bounds. If a player bounces the ball onto any outside line, it is still in play. **(b)** Inside lines are out-of-bounds. If a player hits a ball onto any inside line, that player is out. This applies to all inside lines, not just the lines that border her square.

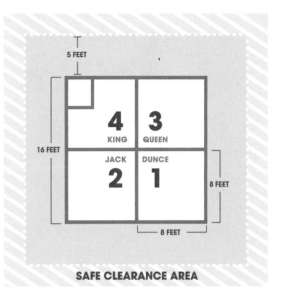

SAFE CLEARANCE AREA

SERVING

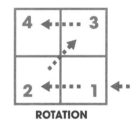

ROTATION

Coach Says . . .

While the classic red playground ball is recommended, a volleyball, soccer ball, or basketball can be used in a pinch. For a real challenge, try to a high-speed game with a tennis ball.

❸ Take your Squares

Players compete for Firsts to decide the first four players and their positions on the square. The first winner of Firsts takes the fourth square, the second winner takes the third square, and so on. If there are remaining players, they must wait outside the court in a line to wait for their chance to enter the game.

Once play begins, players are not required to stay inside their assigned square—they may stand, walk, or run anywhere on the court—though it is best to stay in a position to protect their square.

❹ Serving and returning the ball

The ball is always served from the highest ranked square diagonally across to the lowest square. The server must drop the ball and serve from the bounce. The ball must be allowed to bounce once in the receiving square, then the receiving player must hit the ball into another square of his choice. After the receiver touches the ball, the ball is in play.

Serves are meant to place the ball fairly into play. Because the server must serve the ball the same way each time, it is the receiving player who controls the first play of the game.

⑤ Faults

The receiver of the serve is allowed only one mistake on each round—this is called a fault. If the receiver of the serve hits the ball incorrectly, or fails to hit the ball inbounds, the receiver is allowed to take a second serve. There is only one fault allowed per player per round. This is referred to as "one bad," as in one bad return. However, if a player faults the second time then it's called "two bad." In other words, that is too bad for you, you're out.

Coach Says . . .

If the ball is touched by another object, which is not one of the four players or the floor, this is called interference and the round is started again. Players waiting in line may not touch the ball when it is in play.

⑥ Hitting and possession

During play, players may only hit the ball with their hands. That includes any area between the player's wrists and her fingertips, even the backs of her hands. The ball may be hit with open or closed fists in the same manner as official volleyball—struck once and for a single instant only. Players may not catch, carry or hold the ball at any time during play. Spinning the ball is allowed as long as the hit that produces the spin is not a carry or an illegal hit. In all cases, players who strike the ball incorrectly are eliminated and must exit the game.

Once the ball touches down and bounces in a square, only the owner of the square can touch the ball next—no exceptions. If she does not, then she is out. If she hits it poorly or out of bounds, she is out. If another player hits the ball before she does, at any time, that other player is out.

❼ Elimination

These are all the ways in which a player may be eliminated from the court:

- Failing to hit the ball into another square

- Allowing the ball to bounce more than once in their own square

- Hitting the ball out of bounds or on to an inside line

- Hitting the ball incorrectly, such as holding, catching or carrying

- Hitting the ball with a part of the body other than hands

- Hitting the ball out of turn (also called poaching)

Coach Says . . .

Advancing to the top square comes with the unique privilege of creating special rules. Before serving, the player in the fourth square may invoke special rules, which become part of the game for that one round. After each round, she must call the same rules again or supply new rules, or it is assumed that there are no special rules required in the following round.

Each time a player is eliminated, that player leaves the court and all players advance to the higher numbered square. The lowest ranked square is then filled with a new player. All eliminated players leave the court and wait in line for their turn to rejoin the game in the lowest square.

OPTIONAL RULES

7-Up

Each player that hits the ball must call out a number one higher than the previously called number until seven is reached. The one who is hitting the ball on seven or any number ending in seven must skip that number, yelling "eight" or the next number ending in eight. Failure to do so results in the player being out.

Aerials

Aerials allows the ball to be hit in the air without waiting for it to bounce first.

Around the World

Once invoked, any player in possession of the ball may call around the world regardless of rank at any moment. If it is called, the calling player can hit it to an adjacent square, and that person must hit it to the next adjacent square until it reaches the player who called it, at which point the game returns to normal. Permanent Around the World may be called, in which case the sequence must continue until a player gets out, even if it reaches the caller before then.

Body Hits

The player is allowed to use a specified part of their body to hit the ball (their head or foot for example). Sometimes this rule is called "soccer rules" and the ball may only be hit by the head or foot.

Categories

In this version, the server names a category (e.g., types of drinks, flower names) before play starts, and each player must name something in that category (that nobody has named yet in the round) when they hit the ball. If a player fails to come up with an accurate item in the category, they are out.

Death Rally (a.k.a. Battle, Duel, War, Showdown, and Tea Party)

If the server chooses to allow them, any player may call a death rally. The two players may only hit the ball to each other until one of these two players is eliminated. When a player calls a death rally off at the right moment and quickly puts the ball in another it is called a sneak or stealth attack, and the player who was attacked will often not be able to react to the sudden attack.

Team Duel (a.k.a. Teams)

At any time any player may call duel or teams. They then team up with an adjacent square and play against the other two squares. Such as four and three vs. two and one. The ball may bounce only once in one square, but twice in a team's rectangle. When an out is made both players on the team are out.

Do Over (a.k.a. Redo)

This is used when there is a dispute, players are unsure of a decision, or the line judge determines that the previous play was too close to call or invalidated by an outside interruption. The ball is re-served with no eliminations.

Double Bounces

The ball can (or sometimes must) bounce twice in a player's square before he hits it. If it bounces any other number of times before the receiver hits it, he is out. If it bounces once in and then once out of a player's square, the hitter is out.

Fair Serve (a.k.a. No Blood on Serve)

A common rule in which players cannot get out on the serve. For example, if the server hits the ball out on serve, he is given a second chance; likewise, if a player misses the ball after it is served to him, he also gets a redo.

Final Play (a.k.a. Last Play, Last Round, and Final Rally)

Final play is the term used to denote the last round of play due to the end of the break period. This would usually confirm the winner for the day. Final play could include a duel of the top two squares.

Friendsies

Friendsies allows the players to play balls that did not land in their square and would have otherwise made another player out for the purpose of continuing game play.

Lumberjacks

When a lot of people are playing, have all the extra players spread out around the outside of the court. Those standing around the court are the lumberjacks. When the ball is hit out, the lumberjacks hit the ball back in so the game does not stop. When a player is called out, the remaining players continue playing against each other. The game ends when only one of the four original players remains.

Off-Serve

The player who received service is required to hit the ball back to the server.

Passback

If a player calls "passback" during a game, the next person must hit it back to that player.

Play On

Play on is called when a decision is made to continue play, despite the call being close. Play on must be called immediately by the judge or server after the bounce, or a dispute may occur.

Popcorn

The four square player throws the ball in the air and claps one or more times before catching it. The next player must do the same but with one more clap than the four square player. Each subsequent throw must increase in number of claps, and failure to complete a toss results in an out.

Revenge

When the server gets out, he may choose to call revenge, or king's revenge. The player who is now server must engage in a death rally with the former server (see Death Rally, described earlier).

Sentences

In this version, the server begins a sentence by saying one word, and each play must continue the sentence or end it by saying "period." If they fail to continue the sentence logically, they are out. For example: "I love playing four square period."

Underhand

This means that all hits are with an open hand, palm(s) up. This brings the game down low to the ground and makes your quads ache the next day. Underhand is stereotypically associated with beginners, but in four square even the best players sometimes can't survive a round of underhand.

HITTING TECHNIQUES

This is where the rubber meets the road—or more accurately the hand meets the ball. Hitting technique is one of Four Square's most critical elements. It's what controls accuracy, speed, and ball spin. A player needs to master a full arsenal of hitting choices in order to make the real-time adjustments necessary to hit anything that comes at you with authority. Following are the most common ways to hit the ball.

1 UNDERHAND PUSH

With an upward swing, gently tap the ball with your palm in an underhand fashion. This is a great choice for controlling accurate placement or hitting teardrops.

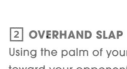

2 OVERHAND SLAP

Using the palm of your hand, slap the ball toward your opponent using an overhand motion. This is a popular and effective method for anyone learning to hit the ball hard.

③ BACKHAND SMACK

Use the backside of your hand to smack the ball in a sideways direction. Backhands are a nice changeup and are great for fake-outs.

④ FORWARD FIST PUNCH

Using a fist, punch through the front of the ball with your knuckles. This method makes it hard to control the ball's accuracy but it makes the ball even harder for your opponent to return if performed right.

⑤ BUMPS

With a fist, hit the ball underhand style to direct the ball toward your opponent. This is an effective method for out of reach and diving hits.

Hitting Styles

SLAMS (a.k.a. high bounces, treetops, cherry bombs)
This style consists of hitting the ball in such a way that it bounces a considerable distance over the receiver's head. More than for being hard to receive, this move is often discouraged for risk of the ball becoming stuck on a roof, in a tree, or rolling into an adjacent game.

SPINNERS (a.k.a. twisters, screwballs, peppermint sticks)
Put some spin on the ball by hitting it off center—influencing both the path and the bounce to make it harder to return.

PSYCHE OUTS (a.k.a. teardrops, babies, Tiny Tims)
A hit where a player acts like he will slam the ball, but instead barely taps it over the line so the other player can't react in time.

Coach Says . . .

Do you have a ball but no court? Just use 1-inch masking tape to mark off squares anywhere you want—it's more accurate than chalk and easier to clean up.

Insider Secrets: Four Square

Because of its many variations and rules, it can sometimes be tough to pin down a proper Four Square strategy—that is, unless you're Sean Effel, cofounder of Four Square World Championships. Follow these tips and play like a king (see what we did there?).

CHANGE UP YOUR HITTING STYLE

There is a huge range of playing styles you can incorporate into Four Square. Effel suggests mixing up your styles in order to stay ahead of the competition. While some players clobber the ball with Godzilla vs. Tokyo strength, other players make short, fast, and tricky Mohammed Ali–style moves to outmaneuver their opponents. "Each end of this spectrum is weak against the other," Effel explains. "It's best to know your fellow players and use a style that works against them."

CHOOSE A POSITION

Effel suggests playing to your strengths when it comes to picking a position. "If zone defense is your thing, position yourself in the rear quarter of the square. You can cover all corners with a minimal amount of footwork and still keep balls from sneaking into your blind spot," he suggests. If a man to man defense is more your thing, you'll be more poised to change your stance depending on which player has the ball. "You move around a lot more, but you are in a better position to return the ball at any given time."

BODY BLOWS

While it may be tempting to get a player out by specifically aiming for a body part *other* than their hand, Effel suggests thinking twice before going for a body blow. "Sometimes this works if a player isn't paying attention, but often it is easy for a player to step out of the way and let the ball sail out of bounds," he warns.

AIR HITS

Since after a hit a ball is allowed to ricochet off players countless times without hitting the ground and still be considered fair, Effel suggests exploiting the heck out of this rule—within reason, of course! Just be sure not to get caught "poaching." And just so it's officially known: a player *is* allowed to leave his square. "You don't have to stand in your own square all the time," Effel explains. "You can stand and run anywhere you want. Just don't leave your square unprotected—someone will get the jump on you."

CRAZY RULES

Being a wild man who lives on the edge, Effel suggests playing Four Square like he lives his life: with no special rules. "I think the simpler the rules of the game, the more fun and flexible it is," Effel says. If you're not the type of person who can live that hard and fast, Effel proposes going for broke with rules that change the very fabric of the game. "Make players literally throw the ball aside and engage in other wacky antics. I love these mini games, and the surprise and chaos that follows right after those rule are tons of fun."

Sean Effel is the cofounder of Boston-based Squarefour, the nation's first four square league. For more information visit SquareFour.org

Big World of Mini Games

Creative players around the world dream up exciting varieties that break out of normal game play entirely. When the ball hits a line (also known as a liner), the players will often call out "liner," and go directly into a mini game before normal play can continue, like one of these that follow.

SHARK ATTACK

The person calling shark attack may hold the ball and run around on the lines to tag another player with the ball, and whoever they tag is eliminated.

BUBBLES

If a player calling liner chooses bubbles, she stands in the intersection, bounces a ball and says "bubbles times (insert number)." The number they call is the amount everyone must let the ball bounce for before normal game proceeds. If the ball is about to stop bouncing, a player may tap it up. After the ball has bounced the said number of times, normal play continues with the player whose court it lands on hitting it next.

ROCKS

If a player chooses rocks, the ball must be bounced hard and slammed into an opponent's court, usually a corner to make it harder. After the hit is completed, normal play proceeds. This is also called footy rucks because it resembles a ruck contest in Australian Rules football.

TAPS

If a player calls liner and chooses taps, they place the ball on the line; at that point, any player can run up and lightly tap the ball to any other players square to begin normal play.

TEA PARTY

The player who was meant to return the liner can call a tea party against the hitter. When this occurs, the match becomes an intense bout between these two players until one is eliminated.

OTHER WAYS TO PLAY

Paddleball-Four Square

This version involves two paddleball sets. Each player uses their wood paddle to hit the small rubber ball in a similar manner as traditional Four Square. The biggest difference being that the ball cannot touch the ground.

Doubles Four Square

If there are a lot of kids and only one ball, this is way to get more people into the game. Four teams of two compete like tag team partners: one teammate is in the square, one is outside of it. After the teammate touches the ball, they switch positions. If they are eliminated, both teammates must go to the end of the line.

Team Four Square

This version takes the game outside the lines—literally. Redraw an 8-ft by 8-ft square court. Each square is now played by three to four teammates each. The rest of the rules still apply, but now there are more people sharing the game.

Tennis Ball Four Square

All of the regular Four Square rules and structure apply, but this version is played with a tennis ball instead of a playground ball. The game play is considerably faster and misses are more frequent.

Two Square

This version of the game is similar to table tennis. Two players use just two of the squares on the court. The player serves the ball across the court to the opponent who must return it. Only the server earns points and it's usually played to twenty-one.

FUN FACT

According to the *Guinness Book of World Records*, the longest Four Square marathon lasted for 29 hours and was played by several students from Buenos Aires in 2008.

The Playground Ball 101

ALSO KNOWN AS: Cherry Ball, Utility Ball, Red Ball
USES: Four Square, Kickball, Dodgeball

HISTORY
Before this ball's invention in the late 1940s, Kickball, Dodgeball, and other games were played with different—often harder—balls. But this new universal ball allowed kids to transition seamlessly from game to game. Its popularity was so dramatic that a 1953 *Los Angeles Times* article claimed that it was pushing games like King of the Mountain and Duck on the Rock into obscurity.

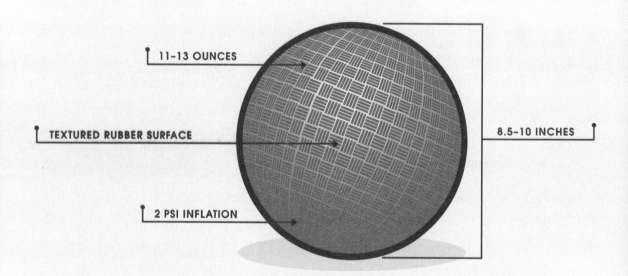

11-13 OUNCES

TEXTURED RUBBER SURFACE

8.5-10 INCHES

2 PSI INFLATION

KICKBALL
A School Yard Staple—This Game Is Like Baseball, but with Your Feet

WHAT IT IS:

Kickball was invented in 1917 specifically to teach baseball strategy to children without the added complication of teaching them how to throw, catch, pitch, or hit a baseball. It was designed as a game that doesn't require very much skill to play, since almost anyone can run, kick, and throw a big rubber ball. And since it requires a large number of players, Kickball is the ultimate game to play with the whole class—without leaving anyone on the bench. Not to mention it offers the unique satisfaction of kicking the heck out of a ball and sending it flying. No wonder, this is one game adults are picking up all over again.

WHAT'S THE POINT?

Kickball consists of two teams, bases, and a big red ball. Played like baseball, the object is to score more runs than the opposing team within five innings.

HOW YOU PLAY

1 Create a field

Take four of your base markers and set them up so that the playing area resembles a baseball diamond. As in baseball, you'll have a home base, first base, second base, and third base. Each base should be twenty paces away from the next. Finally, use the last base marker as a pitching mound set in the middle of the diamond, set about fourteen paces in front of home base.

2 Take the field

Pick teams then choose which team gets Firsts, using any of the First techniques on page 14. The team that wins Firsts gets to be the home team and chooses whether they want to kick first or field first. If they decide to kick first, the away team takes the field. Each base should be manned by a

Game Stats

STYLE: Ball and base game
PLAYERS: Five minimum per team—the more the merrier
REQUIREMENTS:
One large ball
Four base markers (jackets, hats, and that sort of thing will work in a pinch)
Field or clear blacktop
SKILLS:
Kicking
Speed
Agility
Throwing
Stiff toes

- - - - - - - - -

ALSO KNOWN AS
Base Soccer
Soccer Baseball

FUN FACT

Kickball was invented in 1917 by Nicholas C Seuss, the supervisor of park playgrounds in Cincinnati, Ohio.

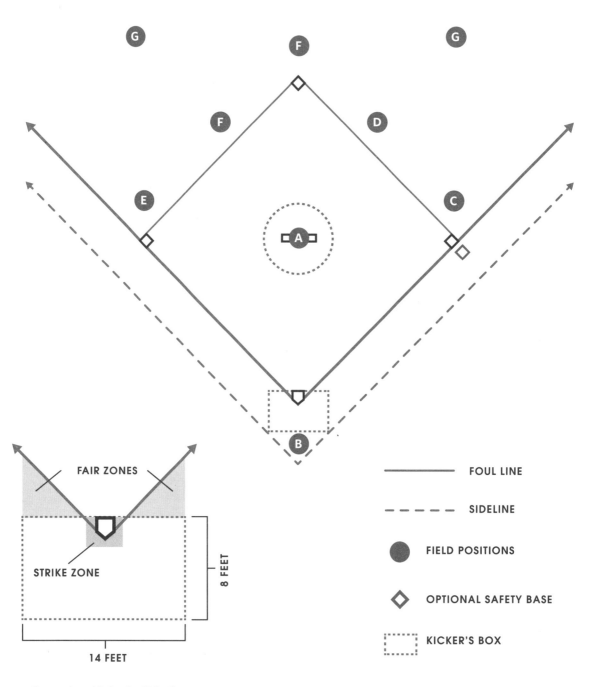

FAIR ZONES

STRIKE ZONE

8 FEET

14 FEET

FOUL LINE

- - - - - - SIDELINE

FIELD POSITIONS

OPTIONAL SAFETY BASE

KICKER'S BOX

Grounders kicked within the
KICKER'S BOX that travel
through the FAIR ZONES and
remain in fair territory are fair.

player so that there is **(A)** a pitcher, **(B)** a catcher, **(C)** a first baseman, **(D)** a second baseman, and **(E)** a third baseman. Any extra players should be **(F)** short fielders, or **(G)** outfielders that cover the area just past first, second, and third baselines.

(3) Batter . . . er, um, kicker up!

The game begins when the first player on the home team steps up to home base. The pitcher on the away team pitches to the kicker by rolling the ball toward him as quickly or as slowly as he sees fit. The pitcher's goal is to get the ball to go over the strike zone—the 2 × 2 square that surrounds and encompasses home base—and safely to the catcher without the player being able to kick it. The kicker, of course, is trying to kick the ball before it rolls into the catcher's hands.

(4) Swing, kicker kicker, swing!

If the kicker manages to kick the ball (any contact with the leg below the knee is considered a kick), he has to run to first base as quickly as possible before someone on the away team can manage to get the ball to the first baseman. If the kicker makes it to first base before anyone on the away team has control of the ball, he can choose to run to the next base.

(5) Not so fast, kicker!

Once the ball is in play, the away team must focus on getting the kicker, or any other base runners, out. They can do this one of several ways:

- The kicker pops the ball into the air and a fielder catches it before the ball touches the ground.

- By forcing the kicker out—this happens when a fielder has the ball and is able to tag the base the kicker is running to before the kicker actually gets there.

- The kicker is touched by the ball in any way while not being on base.

- A kicker runs outside the designated baseline while running from one base to another.

6 Swing and a miss

If the kicker isn't successful at kicking the ball, he's issued one of two things: a strike or a ball.

- **A STRIKE** occurs when the ball rolls over the strike zone or when the kicker attempts to kick the ball and misses. If a kicker gets three strikes while it's his turn at the plate, he is out.

- **A BALL** occurs when the kicker doesn't attempt to kick the ball and the ball manages to stay outside of the strike zone. If a kicker racks up four balls, he gets to walk to first base without any threat of the fielders throwing or tagging him out.

7 Kick through the line up

A kicker continues to kick until he is either **(a)** out or **(b)** on base. After either of those things happens, the next kicker on the home team steps up to the plate to do the same thing, with the goal of getting on base and advancing any base runners on the field.

8 Run the bases

This process continues, with each kicker trying their best to kick the ball in a way that makes it difficult for the fielders to retrieve it. A kicker is allowed to advance from one base to the next as long as he is not tagged out.

9 Runs kicked in

The ultimate goal is for each kicker to go, in order, from first base, to second base, to third base, and then back to home base to score. Once a player successfully tags home base, they score a point, called a "run." However, if three kickers on one team are tagged out, then that half-inning is over and it's the home team's turn to take the field while the away team kicks and attempts to score runs. Once the away team accrues three outs that inning is over, and the next inning begins with the home team kicking once again.

ADDITIONAL RULES

Stick to the Baseline

When running from base to base, players must stay within the baseline—that is, the direct invisible (but sometimes visible) line connecting one base to the other. If a player goes off that line, it's an automatic out.

Double-Bounce Pitches

All pitched balls must bounce at least twice before making their way to home plate. When they do reach the plate, the ball is still allowed to bounce, however, it may not bounce any higher than 12 inches off the ground.

Pegging

Unlike in baseball, Kickball offers a fun (and, depending how you do it, funny) way to get a player out: pegging the runner. Pegging, as discussed in some other games in this book, is basically tagging a player with the ball by throwing it at him. In Kickball, fielders are allowed to tag a player out by throwing the ball right at the runner while he is between bases. If the runner is hit, he's out. Be careful, though, if a player attempts to peg a runner and misses, the ball may fly out of reach of any other fielders, allowing the runner to advance farther.

Foul Balls

If a kicked ball lands beyond the first or third baseline, it's considered a foul ball. Unlike in baseball, a foul ball in Kickball is not considered a strike, however, four foul balls is an out.

Tagging Up

If a fielder catches a fly ball, the kicker is out. However, base runners have the option to "tag up" and try to get extra bases. To tag up, the base runner must tag the base he was on just after the fielder catches the ball. Once he tags up, he has the chance to go for the next base if he thinks he can make it before the ball gets there.

No Leading Off

Unlike in baseball, leading off base in order to get a head start is forbidden in Kickball. Any player who's not on base when the ball is kicked is automatically out.

No Stealing

Another baseball strategy that's frowned upon in Kickball is stealing bases. Anyone attempting to go to another base during pitches is automatically out.

Overthrows

If a fielder attempts to throw a ball to another fielder and over throws it—that is, throws it past a fielder in a way that sends the ball into the outfield or foul territory—the base runners are allowed to continue running the bases at their own risk. Just make sure you get to that next base before the fielders get their hands back on the ball!

Getting a Runner Out

Yes, pegging someone with the ball seems like it's probably one of the funniest ways to get a runner out, but should you do it? Probably not. Even for those with the best aim, hitting a moving target is pretty difficult, especially if the moving target is a human being who is totally expecting it. In most cases, the best way to get a runner out is the old-fashioned way: throw the ball to the player closest to the runner or closest to the base the runner is heading toward. If you're really in a jam (or the temptation is just too great) and you have to peg a player, the best approach is to do it from behind. Not only are they less likely to expect it, but they won't be able to zig and zag, as they're required to stay on the baseline while running.

Coach Says . . .

Next time you're up, try using one of these recess-approved heckles to put some shake into your opponents' knees. Or, if you're feeling saucy, create one of your own and add it to this list!

1. [Point at fielder] This is going for your head!
2. Do you smell some rubber burning?
3. Time for your spanking!
4. Here comes the rain!
5. Hot stuff, coming through!

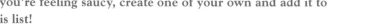

Insider Secrets: Kickball

Whether you roll in soccer style or prefer to go pointy toe, everyone has their own tricks and techniques for dominating Kickball—that includes David Lowry, cofounder of the World Adult Kickball Association. According to Lowry, conquering kickball comes down to practice, patience, and most importantly, fun. The following steps will help you do all three:

KICKIN' BALL

Great Kickball skills start at the feet and . . . well, they stay there. The game is called Kickball after all. But according to Lowry, winning at Kickball is all about keeping the ball low and making sure it doesn't float in the air. "When that happens, the ball tends to hang in the air long enough for a fielder to get under it and catch it," he explains. To avoid the float, don't hit the ball head-on with your toes. Instead, try hitting it with the inside or top of your foot. "If you can connect with that kick regularly—driving the ball more forward than up—you'll be producing hard grounders and line drives which make you a tough out."

PRACTICE MAKES PROFESSIONAL

Lowry recommends playing in as many different leagues as possible, and against as many different teams as possible. "Every team and league has its own personality and a different way of playing the game. You can always learn from another team—even if it's a team you are beating." To further your Kickball education, Lowry also recommends participating in tournaments—or, if that's not an option, at least going to watch one. There's a lot to learn by watching pros do what they do best.

MOST IMPORTANTLY . . .

"Have fun—it's just a Kickball game," says Lowry. Still, if you're looking for an additional nugget of professional Kickball wisdom, he suggests repeating the same mantra his team teaches to all their rookies: Run aggressively, throw conservatively. A team needs a good amount of seasoning to be able to effectively curb a running game, and nothing blows a game open like a miss-throw on a play there was no chance to make.

David Lowry is the cofounder and owner of the World Adult Kickball Association (WAKA). For more information visit Kickball.com.

UNDERHAND

PITCHING TECHNIQUES

While most players may prefer the very natural underhanded "bowling" style of Kickball pitching, an overhand or side-armed approach is the way to pitch like a pro.

Pitching overhand or side-arm not only allows the pitcher to follow the rules of the game, it also helps achieve a variety of high-velocity throws and trick pitches that can devastate the competition.

Take some time to see which throwing style is right for you. By practicing both overhand and side-armed throws, you'll quickly learn how to toss the ball with some spin and twists that will smoke the kicker where he stands!

OVERHAND / SIDE-ARM

KICKING TECHNIQUES: HOW TO KICK THE BALL IN 10 EASY STEPS

1 Be patient
Don't kick at bouncy, off-center, lopsided garbage. Wait—and wait some more.

2 Pick the best pitch
You know it when you see it—straight, even bounce, headed right for your laces.

3 Inhale
Remember to take a deep breath to fill up on oxygen to prepare your body for the adrenaline rush that comes with a well-placed kick.

4 Stance on the ground
Line up to the side opposite your kicking leg. If you kick with your right leg, line up behind home plate and to the left. This will give your leg the proper room to make a powerful swing.

⑤ Run, don't walk

A slight two-step run-up will impart maximum power with minimal actual running.

⑥ Overshoot the base

Just before striking the ball, firmly plant your nonkicking foot with your toes pointing toward the area you want the ball to travel. This sets up your kicking foot to kick through the ball in the correct direction.

⑦ Make contact

The part of your foot you use to hit the ball with will determine how the ball will travel.

⑧ Follow through

Your kicking foot should keep moving forward and in an upward trajectory. Your back foot may have to hop a little to keep you from eating dirt.

⑨ Exhale

We should have said it sooner, but honestly there were more important points to cover. You can breathe when the season's over!

⑩ Run like the wind

As we've seen, a kickball is more than a handful to handle, so assume just about any kicked ball might result in a hit. In other words, less admiring of your now orbiting meteor and more running full speed ahead to first base.

Coach Says . . .

When getting ready to make contact, remember to keep your non-kicking foot planted firmly on the ground and pointed toward the direction you want the ball to travel. Check out the Aiming Techniques section to help you with placement choices before kicking the ball.

Where the Rubber Meets the Foot

Kicking involves a lot more than simply making contact with the ball. Here's a rundown of the kicking styles you should master:

INSTEP
Hitting the ball using the inside of your foot allows for the most control and keeps the ball low making it harder to catch.

SIDE VIEW   TOP VIEW

LACES
Using the top of your foot or "laces" is best for stronger and long-distance shots. However when using your laces, the ball may loft up and float if not struck properly, making it easy to catch.

SIDE VIEW   TOP VIEW

TOE
Hitting the ball directly with the front part of your toes is very hard to control so it's best for bunts and short grounders.

SIDE VIEW   TOP VIEW

OUTSIDE
Although difficult to master, properly hitting the ball with the outside of your foot will create amazing curves, making it very difficult to defend.

SIDE VIEW   TOP VIEW

AIMING TECHNIQUES

When it's your turn to kick, take a look at the game before deciding how and where to kick. How many outs are there? How many runners are on base and what bases are they on? Is the second baseman picking his nose or staring at you with cobra-like focus? Are the outfielders playing close or far? All of these factors should play into how and where you kick the ball. Following are some common situations in Kickball and the best way to kick your way out of them:

- Nobody on base: Whether you're kicking first, earlier kickers have already scored, or the first two players already popped out, kicking a fair ball on the ground down the third baseline is the way to go. This keeps the ball as far away from your destination (first base) as possible, while ensuring the fielders can't catch it in the air for an instant out.

- Runner on first, no outs: If you have a runner on first, the most important thing you can do as a kicker is to help her advance to the next base, no matter what. This is when you pull a sacrifice kick. Aim the kick as a weak ground dribbler between the pitcher's mound and first base. This will cause the pitcher and first baseman to scurry for the ball. Once they get it, the closest and easiest out for them to get will be the kicker running for first—allowing the runner going toward second to arrive safely at the base.

- Runner on third (and/or second): With runners in scoring position, try to kick the ball between first and second base. This will give the player on third more time to run to home base as the fielders will likely be trying to tag out the player at first, since that's their best bet.

How to Be an All-Star Catcher

The catcher has one of the most important jobs in Kickball: to make sure nobody scores a run. To do this, they need to play a little differently from the rest of the fielders in order to make sure nobody sets foot in their house. Following are some things to remember when guarding the plate.

PERFECT YOUR THROWING AND CATCHING SKILLS

It's up to the catcher to make sure that any nonkicked balls always end up back with the pitcher. This means catching and throwing the ball just right, as missing a catch or over throwing a ball back to the pitcher could result in a loose ball, giving runners an opportunity to advance.

NEVER LEAVE YOUR POST

When a kicker hits a weak kick that stays nearby, it may be tempting to go after the errant ball, but doing so could leave home base wide open to a runner advancing from second or third. Instead, let the pitcher go after those balls—she doesn't have an important base to protect like you do.

DON'T WATCH *JUST* THIRD BASE

The biggest threat to a catcher comes from the runner at third base, but that doesn't mean trouble can't come from elsewhere. A good catcher keeps tabs on all the bases, making sure he's ready for any threat that may arise.

NEVER TRY TO PEG A RUNNER

While it may seem like an easy shot, it's always a bad idea for the catcher to peg a runner coming in from third base. The runner could easily duck under the ball, meaning he'll then be able to score a run without any opposition. Instead, hold the ball tight, dig your feet into the ground and . . .

BLOCK THE PLATE

It's up to the catcher to make sure nobody sets foot on home base—if that means standing in front of a quickly charging runner, then so be it. Just make sure you have possession of the ball, otherwise you're not allowed to block the base- line. Hey, nobody ever said this was easy!

What's Fair? What's Foul?

Because Kickball is a game of many moving parts (and, to be honest, lots of rules to keep things honest) it can get pretty tricky to keep track of what kicks are in fair play and which are foul balls. Since four foul balls equal one out, it's pretty important to know the difference.

Following is a rundown of the various scenarios (courtesy of the World Adult Kickball Association):

A FOUL BALL OCCURS WHEN:

- A kicked ball that first touches the ground in foul territory, even if it enters fair territory after doing so

- A kicked ball that first touches a fielder standing entirely in foul territory, while the ball is over foul territory

- A kicked ball lands in fair territory, but touches the ground in foul territory on its own at any time before crossing the first or third baseline

- A kicked ball lands in fair territory, then enters foul territory before crossing the first or third baseline, and touches a fielder or entirely in foul territory

- A kick made on or above the knee of the kicker

- A kicked ball touched more than once or stopped in the kicking box by the kicker

- A kicked ball that is kicked from outside of the kicking box

- A kicked ball that first touches a permanent object around the field (e.g., a bleacher, a batting cage, a fence)

To be fair, that's a lot of potential for foul balls. Fortunately, what counts as a fair ball is much simpler to understand.

A FAIR BALL OCCURS WHEN:

- A kicked ball lands and remains in fair territory

- A kicked ball lands in fair territory, then travels into foul territory beyond the first or third baseline

- A kicked ball that touches a player in fair territory

- A kicked ball lands in fair territory, then touches a player in fair territory before touching the ground in foul territory

- A kicked ball touches a runner before touching the ground in foul territory

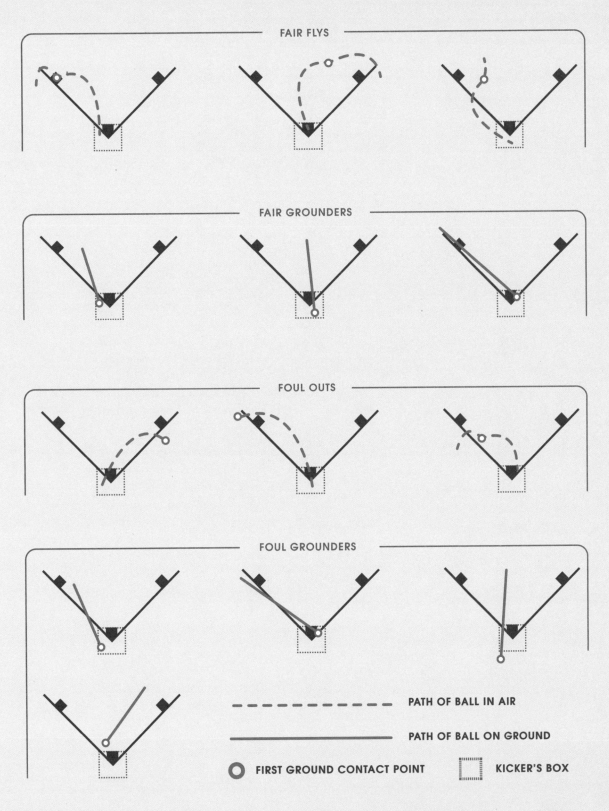

FAIR FLYS

FAIR GROUNDERS

FOUL OUTS

FOUL GROUNDERS

- - - - - - - - PATH OF BALL IN AIR

————————— PATH OF BALL ON GROUND

○ FIRST GROUND CONTACT POINT   KICKER'S BOX

Am I Out?

There is a definitive explanation of what is and isn't considered an out in Kickball. But many wars have started and many friendships have ended, all because of three words: "I'm not out!"

In Kickball, three outs mean the end of an inning for each team, which makes it a crucial part of the game that can make all the difference between winning and losing. Because of that, knowing what actually is and is not an out is imperative to keeping things fair, honest, and civilized. To help determine what is and is not considered an out, we've put together this handy definitive guide, thanks to help from the World Adult Kickball Association.

AN OUT OCCURS WHEN:

- A kicker racks up a count of three strikes or four fouls

- Any kicked ball (fair or foul) is caught by a fielder before the ball hits the ground. Any part of the ball may incidentally touch the ground during the act of catching and still be ruled an out if the fielder can prove she has full control of the ball and maintains control after it touches the ground.

- A fielder accomplishes a "force out," which is when a fielder is holding the ball and has any part of her body on the base to which a runner is being forced to run. The fielder must be touching the base before the runner arrives at the base. It's okay if the ball is touching the ground as long as the fielder can show she has full control of the ball while still tagging the base. If it appears to be a tie, the favor goes to the runner.

- A runner is touched by the ball at any time while not on base while the ball is in play

- A kicker or runner interferes with the ball

- A fielder tags a base while in possession of the ball just after a runner has left that base, but before he's had the opportunity to "tag up" after a fly ball has been caught

- A runner is off base when the ball is kicked

- A kicker takes a turn before it's her turn in the lineup

- A runner passes the runner ahead of them

- A runner strays outside of the baseline

- A runner passes a base without tagging it

- A runner fails to properly tag up on a caught fly ball

- A runner is tagged by the ball while going from one base to another

- A player is hanging out on the sidelines during the game when he's not supposed to be there

WIFFLE BALL
An American Classic for over Six Decades

Game Stats

STYLE: Bat and ball game
PLAYERS: Four or more
REQUIREMENTS:
Wiffle ball
Wiffle bat
Strike zone
Field
SKILLS:
Throwing
Catching
Hand-eye coordination

FUN FACT

The original spelling of "Wiffle" was actually "Whiffle." The "h" was dropped when it was time to make the building's sign. The reason: It cost too much for another letter!

WHAT IT IS

Wiffle Ball is one of the most beloved American pastimes. Now played around the world, in backyards and culs-de-sac, at family picnics and birthday parties, Wiffle Ball is for players from ages 6 to 106. With its inexpensive equipment (one ball, one skinny yellow bat, one open space) and its wide appeal, Wiffle Ball is maybe the most underrated game of all-time. But don't let its simplicity be mistaken as simplistic. Wiffle Ball can take a lifetime to master—or at least a few summers.

WHAT'S THE POINT?

Wiffle Ball has all the fun of baseball distilled into a perfect competition of tricky pitches and speedy home runs. Base-running and the huge lineups are done away with, leaving just you, your best buds, and a slim chance of breaking anything you're not supposed to.

HOW YOU PLAY
Set up the Ballpark

A Wiffle field is basically a narrow triangle. The main idea is to make home runs commonplace, so you don't want the field to be too long. The distance from home plate and the home-run "wall" should only be about 85 feet (more or less depending on everyone's skill level). Home-run walls can be made out of anything: a fence, a sidewalk, a roof, or any other easily defined area. The width of the home-run wall shouldn't be too wide either, anywhere from 50–100 feet (narrower if playing with fewer players).

The rest of the triangle is broken up into three main hitting zones, **A** triples zone, **B** doubles zone, and **C** singles zone as shown in the diagram opposite.

When marking off the hitting areas, use landmarks like trees and rocks or place hats, shoes, cones, or other clear markers to designate the hitting areas and foul lines.

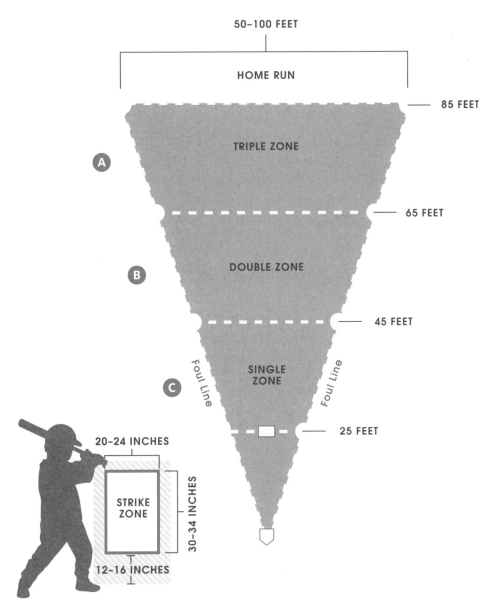

The pitching "mound" should be centered on the front line of the single zone for beginners or the front line of the double zone for experts (or anywhere in between).

Choose Your Teams

You need at least two players per team so each team has a pitcher and a fielder. You can have up to five players per team, but both teams need to have the same number of players.

FUN FACT

The Wiffle Ball was invented in 1953 as a solution to a burgeoning sporting challenge—how to throw a wicked curve ball. There was an added benefit to this light plastic ball: it was the perfect game to play in close quarters without damaging any property or going too far to chase after the ball.

Play Ball!

Games are played in six innings. Each team gets one at bat per inning. The batting order stays the same throughout the game. When playing the field, players take turns pitching, alternating at the beginning of each inning. Each team gets three outs per inning. An out for the batter can be made in three ways:

1 THREE STRIKES EQUAL ONE OUT.
A strike occurs when: **(a)** The ball hits the strike zone and the batter doesn't swing, **(b)** the batter swings and completely misses the ball (a.k.a. a whiff), **(c)** the batter hits the ball into foul territory. Fouls and foul tips count as a strike for the first two strikes only. A batter cannot strike out on a foul or foul tip, they have unlimited foul balls.

2 ANY FLY BALL CAUGHT IN FAIR OR FOUL TERRITORY.

3 GROUND BALLS FIELDED IN FAIR TERRITORY WHILE THE BALL IS IN MOTION. Ground balls can be bobbled, but if the ball hits the ground in fair territory, it's a single. Once a ground ball enters fair territory, it's an automatic hit. Bunting is not allowed.

Scoring

There is no actual base running in Wiffle Ball. Players use their imagination to run the bases and keep track—this is called ghost running. Ghost runners advance on base when they hit the ball as follows:

- If a player is pitched five balls (nonstrike pitches) before striking out, the player gets a walk and advances to first base. Hit batters do not take a base.

- If the ball is grounded or hit into the single zone and isn't caught, the player gets a single and advances to first base

- If the ball is hit into the double zone and isn't caught, the player gets a double and advances to second base

- If the ball is hit into the triple zone and isn't caught, or the ball hits the home-run wall and isn't caught off the bounce, the player gets a triple and advances to third base

- If the ball lands over the home-run wall, the player scores with a home run

When ghost runners reach a base, they advance on additional hits as follows:

- All runners score on a home run

- A runner on first base advances one base on a single, two bases on a double, and scores a run on a triple

- A runner on second base stays on a single, scores on a double or a triple

- A runner on third base scores on any hit

Game Over

The game ends after six innings and the team with the most runs wins. A ten-run lead mercy rule is in effect after three full innings of play. In case of a tie, additional innings can be played until one team has more runs at the end of a full inning.

The Strike Zone

Wiffle Ball players don't have the luxury of endless teammates and million-dollar equipment, so when it comes to filling the catcher position, you need to get creative. Having a physical strike zone can help determine if the pitch is a ball or a whiff, and removes the need for an umpire or arguments about who saw what. Here are your best choices:

LAWN CHAIR
Pro: Backrest provides perfect and consistent strike zone, readily available at outdoor functions, may catch some strikes, keeping ball retrieval to a minimum.
Con: Can be temperamental in windy conditions, may be commandeered by elderly relatives for seating.

COOLER
Pro: The open lid, when positioned correctly, provides an appropriate strike zone and keeps refreshments close by.
Con: Hard bounces make strikes harder to chase down and you risk constant interference from people looking for drinks.

BABY STROLLER
Pro: Provides a consistent strike zone, the seat area is better than average at catching balls, easy to position.
Con: The baby or parents of said baby might try to interfere with the game.

OPTIONAL RULES
Double Plays
A double play may be attempted at any time, regardless if there are runners on base. Any fielded ball (ground ball or pop fly) can be thrown to the strike zone. If the throw hits the strike part of the zone in the air, the team on the field gains two outs. No runners are removed from the bases.

PITCHING TECHNIQUES
The best thing about throwing a Wiffle Ball is, of course, the exaggerated movement required to get the ball up to speed. Thanks to the ball's design, pitching a Wiffle Ball will have you throwing like a pro in no time. The most important factor of a great pitch is the grip. Wiffle Ball pitching employs a great arsenal of grips that need to be mastered and practiced so that you too can control the power of the Wiffle. You don't need to throw the ball hard, you just need to master these grips and perfect your release. Study the illustrations, practice hard, and get ready to strike out anyone who steps up to the plate.

Coach Says . . .

Before you try a new pitch, scuff your ball. You'll get more movement on your pitches. Experiment with rubbing your new Wiffle balls with sandpaper (sixty grit is preferred) on an asphalt driveway, or on a concrete sidewalk. The advantage to scuffing is that it adds a little more consistency and jazzy movement to your balls, and it keeps your hands from slipping off the pristine plastic and throwing off your pitch.

The Fastball (a.k.a. The Straight Shooter, Mr. Easy, Straight-Up)

The fastball is the easiest pitch to throw in the game. To grip, place holes facing home plate and the tips of the index and middle fingers over the top holes. With the thumb on the bottom seam of the ball, place your ring finger and pinky together along the top seam of the ball. Don't grip the ball too tight—a nice loose grip is more effective. And thankfully, this grip is the same for righties and lefties.

The Curveball: (a.k.a. Bread & Butter, The Big Secret, Watch Your Head)

This pitch is the reason the Wiffle ball was invented. For right-handed pitchers, place the holes facing out. The middle finger should be placed just to the left of the holes. The index finger is spread about two inches from the middle finger, like making the hippie sign for peace. The thumb is placed on the bottom of the ball along the seam and in the area in the middle of the two fingers. The ring finger and the pinky finger are together and against the center of the ball. Again a loose grip is very effective. Left-handed pitchers grip the ball the same, only opposite.

The Screwball (a.k.a. Slider, Break Dancer, Chuck Sheen)

The screwball grip is the opposite of the curveball grip. Spokes are kept in for the right-handed pitchers. Keep your index finger on the seam of the ball. Your ring finger and pinky (the petites) are touching the solid portion of the ball. Your thumb will stay along the seam as well. This grip gets a loose one and the pitch is thrown over the top. If you are a left-handed pitcher you will need to flip the grip.

The Knuckleball (a.k.a. Crazy Eye, The Swivel, Bare Handed Beast)

This pitch is a rarity in the Wiffle world due to its difficulty to control. The grip requires supreme digital dexterity. The holes of the ball face home plate and the fingernails of the index finger and middle finger should dig into the ball on the seam. The thumb should be on the bottom seam of the ball and the ring and pinky fingers should be together. A very tight grip is recommended, but crushing the ball could result in a delay of the game. This grip is ambidextrous.

The Riser:
(a.k.a. High Rise, Up 'n' At 'Em, Get Up)
The Riser defies gravity. If thrown right, the
ball should start at the batter's toes and end
up at their nose. You want to throw this pitch
side-arm, keeping your wrist straight. Perfo-
rations stay parallel to the ground. Keep your
index and middle fingers above the seam of
the ball with a tighter than usual grip. Your
ring finger and pinky may tuck underneath to
reduce drag. Get as low as possible and begin
the side-arm action, with wrist straight, and
release with a violent snap! The ball should
rise a good several feet.

**The Sinker: (a.k.a. The Drop, The All-Pro,
Good Luck)**
The sinker is the most difficult pitch to throw
and is feared by every hitter in the lineup.
The holes face skyward with the index finger
along the equatorial seam. The middle finger
is spread two inches from the index finger.
The thumb is on the seam of the ball and the
ring finger and the pinky finger are together
and touching the solid part of the ball. This
pitch sinks hard on both right-handed and
left-handed batters—in other words, dropping it like it's hot. This pitch is very hard
on a pitcher's arm and is *not* recommended
for younger pitchers to throw. Use this pitch
sparingly for maximum effect.

Insider Secrets: Wiffle Ball

If you don't take the time to appreciate the Wiffle Ball's unique throwing style, your pitching is going to have more holes than the ball itself. Follow these tips from Nick Benas, President of The Wiffle Ball Player's Association, and you'll be able to have batters swinging at empty air.

VARY YOUR PITCHING DELIVERY

According to Benas, batters are all but counting on you to pitch with the same timing each time, so throw them a monkey wrench by changing things up. "Learn to start throwing with a step to the left, a step to the right, as well as a step out in front and slide step to throw off your batter," says Benas. Doing so will take some getting used to, but it will pay off.

DON'T OVER DO IT.

Pitching a Wiffle Ball can be tough on your body, so make sure you practice good form and keep your body strong. "When you pitch, stay long on the ball instead of using small short choppy motions—wrist action is the key," says Benas, who also suggests lengthening your stride on the delivery to further prevent injury.

KEEP AN EYE ON THE HOLES

Want to predict how a batter is going to hit the ball? Benas suggests you watch the holes. "Wherever those holes are pointed upon release, the ball is going to fly in the opposite direction, because of how the air flows through the ball." He adds that you'll want to keep the ball spinning on a perfect axis (with holes lined up with each other) when you snap your wrist.

Nick Benas is President of The Wiffle Ball Player's Association and CEO of Big League Wiffle Ball. For more information visit BigLeagueWiffleball.com.

STICKBALL
The Crown Jewel of Urban Sport

WHAT IT IS
Stickball is both old school and new school. Stickball came on the scene when kids started sawing off their mothers' broom and mop handles to use as bats back in the early 1800s, a tradition that exists still to this day. The game harkens back to when life was simple, when games were homegrown and played in the city streets of New York City, Philadelphia, and Boston. These geographical hot spots provided the ultimate in ethnic diversity, and neighborhoods would battle each other in legendary pickup games.

WHAT'S THE POINT?
With a bunch of friends, a stick, a rubber ball, and a quiet street (or empty playground or parking lot) you can have a full day of serious fun and intense competition. Just make sure windows are far enough away to be safe from breakage and maybe more importantly, make sure to get home in time for dinner.

HOW YOU PLAY
Make the Field
The ideal field for Stickball is a quiet street, an empty parking lot, or a paved playground. Use cars or fences as foul lines, and fire hydrants, sewer covers, or car bumpers as the bases. The following are the best items to use for bases:

- Parked cars
- Manhole covers
- Fire hydrants
- Parked bikes
- Rolled up jackets

- Baseball caps or other hats
- Chalk (to draw your own)
- Large rocks
- Trash can lids
- Parking cones

Game Stats

STYLE: Bat and ball game
PLAYERS: Two or more
REQUIREMENTS:
Rubber ball
Bat
Chalk
SKILLS:
Throwing
Catching
Hand-eye coordination

- - - - - - - - - -

ALSO KNOWN AS
Streetball

FUN FACT
Baseball Hall of Famer Willie Mays would play Stickball with children in his Harlem neighborhood the mornings of his big league games. He credits Stickball for his being able to hit the breaking-ball pitch in the major leagues.

Stickball Equipment 101

FUN FACT

In the city of Boston, Stickball players are known to cut off the blade of their old hockey sticks to be doubled as a wicked-good Stickball bat.

STICK

2.5 INCHES

BROOMSTICK OR MOP STICK

33–40 INCHES

ELECTICAL TAPE HANDLE

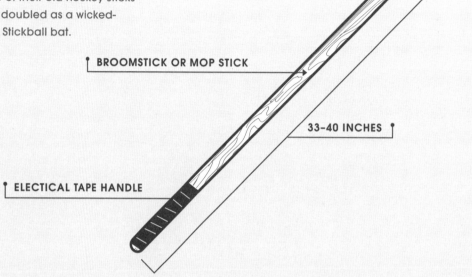

BALL

3 OUNCES

SILKY RUBBER SURFACE

PINK COLOR

2.25 INCHES

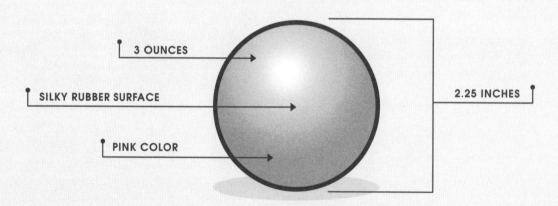

The Great Ball Debate: Spaldeen vs. Pensie Pink

One thing that many of these classic recess games have in common is the ball that was used to play them. While a tennis ball would work, they were usually a little pricey for the young kids who were looking for a good, strong ball that could hold up after hours of play. Thus came the pink rubber ball, an easy-to-find, easy-to-afford piece of equipment that could be used for dozens of games. Two brands of these rubber balls dominated the streets and recess yards: The Spaldeen and the Pensie Pink.

THE SPALDEEN

The Spaldeen was actually a nickname given to the Spalding brand of pink rubber balls—they earned the name Spaldeen because that's how kids speaking with New York City accents would pronounce "Spalding."

Spaldeens were known for having a rougher outside, which made them easier to grip and throw, especially after rolling through a puddle. They were also the most carried brand of rubber balls, meaning kids could find them at just about any drugstore or candy shop in walking distance of their house.

THE PENSIE PINK

The Pensie Pink was created by the Penn Tennis Supply Company to directly compete with the Spaldeen. Much like its competition, the Pensie Pink was made out of the rubber used inside a tennis ball. What made the Pensie stand out was its smoother surface, which added a little more challenge to catching and holding the ball. Many players also felt that the Pensie Pink was a little lighter and had a little more bounce to it.

THE BEST BALL?

There's no clear-cut answer as to which ball is superior. While Spaldeen has more name recognition, there are still a lot of players who will defend the Pensie Pink until the day they die. At the end of the day it's not about the type of ball, it's how you use it.

FUN FACT

Originally discarded rejects for the tennis ball manufacturing process, pink balls were first marketed as soft kid-friendly balls back in the 1950s.

FUN FACT

In the Bronx borough of New York City—the unofficial birthplace of Stickball—there's a street named Stickball Boulevard, which lies between Lafayette and Randall Boulevards.

WORLD OF PLAY

Games with rubber balls dates back to 1400 B.C. when people of Ancient Mexico and Central American played a sport called Ōllamaliztli. While the details are murky, it seemed to involve teams using their hips to hit a solid rubber ball and losers were often times sacrificed to the gods. In other words, a game best left in the history books.

Stickball is a classic and unique game, so of course it has its own way of picking teams and sides. If everyone brings their own stick (they should have!) put everyone's in a pile, like setting up a game of pickup sticks. A volunteer kneels next to the sticks and, with one hand covering his eyes, throws bats to each side to designate teams.

Decide on a Pitching Style

The most important thing to determine before you start playing is how you want to pitch. This depends on where you're playing and how many players you have.

- **FAST PITCH (ALSO KNOWN AS WALLBALL):**
  Usually played with one to three players per team in a yard or lot with a wall or fence as a backstop. A strike zone is drawn on the wall with chalk measuring about 21 inches wide and 28 inches tall and standing 15 inches off the ground. The pitcher stands about 50 feet back and throws the heat. In fast pitch, strikes are as follows:

  - If the ball hits the strike zone, it's a strike

  - If the hitter swings and misses, it's a strike

  - If a ball is hit foul, it's a strike

- **SLOW PITCH (ALSO KNOWN AS BOUNCE PITCHING):**
  Usually played with three to eight players per side in a street setting. The pitchers stands 40 to 50 feet back from the hitter and lobs the ball, allowing it to bounce once before the hitter swings. In slow pitch, strikes are as follows:

  - If the hitter swings and misses, it's a strike

  - If a ball is hit foul, it's a strike

- **FUNGO (ALSO KNOWN AS SELF-PITCH):**
  This style can be played in any setting or location and requires no pitcher. Fungo is probably the most common style of stickball. The batter tosses the ball into the air and then hits it on the way back down or after one or more bounces. Stickball aficionados prefer hitting after one bounce.

Coach Says . . .

Try experimenting with hitting the ball after no bounces, after one, two or, even three bounces. This will throw off the fielders and keep them guessing each time you come up to bat.

Batter Up

The overall concept of Stickball is very similar to baseball. The main difference comes in with the strikes and fouls. In Stickball, hitters are only allowed two strikes (not three) for an out. Foul balls are considered strikes, and batters can strike out on a foul ball (no unlimited foul balls). There are no balls or walks either.

Aside from fouls, strikes, and pitching style, everything else about the game is the same as baseball—players run bases and outs come from catches, tags, force-outs and strikeouts. After three outs teams switch sides.

If the ball gets hit onto a roof, porch, or any area that gets you into trouble, it's an automatic out. If the ball gets lost or can't be retrieved, the game is over.

WORLD OF PLAY

From Australian and England to Pakistan and India, the cricket-playing world has their own version called Bin Cricket. While it often involves a real cricket bat, the stumps are painted on a trash bin that is wheeled around for an instant match.

Home Run Celebration Techniques

There are many ways to rejoice the glory of a home run. The most natural techniques, however, involve the gratuitous use of the stick. Here are just a few of the best celebrations.

The Clean and Jerk
Pretend the bat is a barbell and you're a pumped-up weightlifter. Dramatically raise the bat to the roof.

The Lone Ranger
Straddle the stick like a horse and gallop around the bases as you hoot, holler, and wave one arm in victory.

The Shredder
Hold the stick with the handle raised like the neck of a speed metal guitar and shred the "axe."

The Telescope
Hold the stick up to one eye as you try to locate the bomb you just blasted into space.

Stickball Lingo

If you're going to play the game, then you'd better know the street slang that goes along with it.

ARROW: a straight fastball to the strike zone

CHIN MUSIC: pitches thrown close to the batter's face

CHUCK: a nickname for a pitcher

BARREL: the sweet spot of the bat

CIRCUS CATCH: an acrobatic catch

BASKET CATCH: catching the ball with your finger tips

CLUB: another name for a bat

CYCLE: when a batsman gets a single, double, triple, and homer in a row

DISH: home plate

CAN OF CORN: easy to catch pop-up

FACIAL: getting hit in the face with the ball

CHEESE: junk pitching that's easy to hit

FLINTSTONE: a big over-sized bat

FROZEN ROPE: a straight line drive hit

TABLE SETTER: a leadoff or no. 2 hitter whose job is to get on base

TATER: a home run

TEXAS LEAGUER: a hit that drops in over the middle infielders' heads. Hook 'em horns!

PUNCH OUT: another name for a strikeout

TWINS: double play or to hit for a double

TWIN KILLING: making a double play

UNCLE CHARLIE: black eye from a ball to the face

SHOESTRING CATCH: catching a line drive by your feet

WHEELHOUSE: in the batter's strike-zone sweet spot

SHOT: a nice hit

WHEELS: fast runner

SOUTHPAW: a left-handed pitcher

WORLD OF PLAY

The British Cricketers had a version of Stickball, too. Their cobbled streets were littered with their own versions of the game: Old Cat, Rounder's, Town Ball, and Stoolball. The Canadians called their Stickball "Burby" in the early days, which was a riff on the new suburban landscapes popping up in lightly populated areas.

STOOPBALL
The King of Old School Urban Games

Game Stats

STYLE: Throw and
   catch game

PLAYERS: Three or more

REQUIREMENTS:

A tennis ball, racquetball,
   or a classic pink high-
   bounce ball

A stoop (you can use a
   street curb, too)

Cleared space in front of
   the stoop

Chalk or landmarks (to
   mark for point value)

SKILLS:

Great bouncing skills

Good catching hands

Strong hand-eye
   coordination

- - - - - - - - - - -

ALSO KNOWN AS

Off the Point

Step Ball

Stair Ball

WHAT IT IS

Made popular by kids in big cities, Stoopball is the perfect way to squeeze in a game of baseball without the bases, a bat, or even a diamond. All you need is a rubber ball and some steps. Stoopball gets its name because it was played on the stoops outside of apartment buildings, and houses, in cities. For these kids, especially after World War II, stoops represented a place to hang out and come up with new games, so it makes perfect sense that one of the best games involves these popular hangout points. Fortunately for students today, many schools have similar steps leading to the play yard, so the tradition lives on.

WHAT'S THE POINT?

Stoopball is just like baseball: it has a batter, fielders, and nine innings. The batter throws the ball at the steps so it bounces over his head. The goal is to get the ball to bounce and fly out as far as possible and land in a spot that will grab you the most points. But watch out—the fielders are out there to catch the ball and make sure the batter doesn't get any points. Players take turns at bat each inning. The player with the most runs after nine innings wins.

HOW YOU PLAY

1 Determine the field

Once a stoop is picked, players decide on which parts of the field are fair and which are foul.

2 Batter up!

The person who lives farthest from the steps gets to bat first. The batter stands about three feet in front of the steps, facing it head on. The fielders also face the steps and spread out behind the batter, standing at least 10 feet behind her.

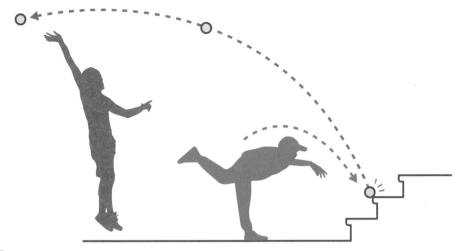

③ The Pitch

The batter throws the ball at the steps. The point is to get the ball to hit it at the perfect angle so the ball bounces over the batter's head and lands in fair territory in order to score runs.

④ Playing the field

It's up to the fielders to catch the ball so the batter doesn't score any runs. If a fielder catches the ball or the ball lands in foul territory, the batter is out. If the ball hits the ground, the batter gets a run for each time the ball bounces before a fielder can get to it.

⑤ Next inning

After the first batter takes her turn, the next player who lives second farthest from the stoop goes to bat. It continues like this until each player gets an at-bat turn. Once every player gets an at-bat, the inning is over. After nine innings, the player with the most runs wins!

Fun Fact

Celebrity fans of Stoopball include Sandy Koufax, Billy Joel, Ad Rock of the Beastie Boys, and Marv Albert, who had a "stoop-to-nowhere" constructed on his property in the suburbs just to satisfy his passion for the game.

Coach Says . . .

Forget your mitts! It may be tempting to bring your baseball glove to a game of Stoopball, but bringing a mitt takes away from the simple fun of the game, which is that you can play it anytime and anywhere with no fuss or muss.

THROWING TECHNIQUES

One of the things that makes Stoopball so much fun is its unpredictability—once you throw the ball against the steps, that thing can go anywhere! But with some skill and some knowledge of simple physics, you can use these bouncing techniques to show the world that you're a Sultan of Stoop!

The Double Bounce

Great for throwing a zippy line drive, the double bounce involves throwing the ball so that it bounces off the step and then immediately bounces off of the wall of the next step up.

The Lip Smack

Looking to achieve maximum air with the ball? Then throw it as hard as you can at the top corner, or lip, of the highest step. When hit right, this will send the ball flying over the fielders' heads and into home-run territory.

The Reflector

Catch the fielders off guard with this low-flying shot that will buzz just over your head. The trick is to aim for the inside corner of the middle steps—that is, that point where two steps connect. This could take some practice depending on the setup, but when done right, this shot will ricochet the ball right back at you and keep your opponents guessing. Just make sure to get out of the way of the ball!

Fun Catches

Everyone can catch a ball, but not everyone can do it with flair. Try these cool, showy, trick catches to wow spectators and fellow players alike.

STATUE OF LIBERTY

A catch you can literally do with one hand tied behind your back, the Statue of Liberty is a great way to look cool while paying tribute to New York City, the original home of Stoopball. To pull it off simply get under the ball, raise a single arm into the air and catch the ball, standing just like that. Pause for a second so everyone can notice and respect the move.

BEHIND THE BACK

As the ball begins its downward trajectory, position yourself under it and lean forward ever so slightly. Cup your hand against your back and let the ball fall right into the area where your hand and back meet. It's a tricky move that takes practice to pull off, but the cheers you get for it will make the whole thing worth your while.

HAT TRICK

Just as the ball begins to come down toward you, pull off your hat and let the ball fall right into it. A simple way to show everyone you're an ace of the Stoopball field.

OFF THE WALL

This maneuver is great for plucking a ball out of the air just before it lands. By jumping with one foot "into" a wall (or parked car), use your foot to push yourself off the wall in order to get some extra height.

EYES CLOSED

Show the batter that he's got nothing on you by holding out your hands and closing your eyes just before the ball lands in your hands. Just make sure you're absolutely positive where the ball is going to land, otherwise you'll have a big pink welt to show for your troubles.

FADE AWAY JUMPER

When a ball is about to land behind a car, take a note from your favorite and do a reverse fading jump backward to give you the extra length needed to turn that hit into an out.

OTHER WAYS TO PLAY
Original Stoopball

Before it became the baseball-inspired modern version often played today, Stoopball was played much differently. This version of Stoopball, sometimes called Original Stoopball, can be played solo or with a small group of friends.

Playing Original Stoopball is simple. The player who is up stands 10 to 15 feet away from the stoop and bounces the ball off of it. The point is to catch the ball and return it as many times as you can, with each type of catch being worth a different amount of points:

- Catching a ball after it bounces once: 5 points
- Catching a fly ball: 10 points
- Catching a pointer (a fly ball that hits the top lip of the step): 100 points

If a player can't catch the ball, that's an out and the next player is up. Players keep taking turns like this until one of them reaches 1,000 points and takes the game.

HANDBALL
A Schoolyard Version of the Classic Game

WHAT IT IS

While the term "handball" is used to describe a lot of different games, there's only one that truly matters: the one that you can play against the wall with some pals in the recess yard. Handball is a fun mashup of racquetball and volleyball. The game is like racquetball in that it involves bouncing a ball off the wall. It's like volleyball because your goal is to get points by making sure nobody can return the ball. As with both games, some quick thinking and hotshot ball-bouncing skills are going to be what separates the champs from the chumps.

WHAT'S THE POINT?

Handball is a little different from other wall games because the main focus is ensuring your opponents can't keep the ball moving after it bounces off the wall. Play by bouncing the ball off the wall in such a way that your opponent won't be able to get to the ball and do the same thing. Every time this happens, you get a point. The first player or team to get twenty-one points wins.

HOW YOU PLAY

❶ Serve time

Whoever has Firsts serves by bouncing the ball off of the floor, then smacking it or punching it into the wall. (You're not allowed to catch or throw the ball).

❷ Bounce and return

After the ball bounces off the wall, it's up to the other players to try and smack the ball back at the wall. Once the ball bounces off the wall, players can either let the ball bounce off the ground once, or they can smack it on the fly right after the ball returns from its bounce against the wall.

Game Stats

STYLE: Throw and catch game

PLAYERS: Two (to play one-on-one) or four (to play doubles)

REQUIREMENTS:

A wall

A tennis ball or racquetball

SKILLS:

Strong hands

Fast feet

Catlike reflexes

③ Playing defense

Only the server or serving team can score points during a round, so it's up to the other players to make sure they return the ball after each bounce. If a player messes up and they either can't hit the ball or can't bounce it off the wall, the server then scores a point and gets to serve again.

④ Switch it up

It's time to switch servers when: **(a)** the current server messes up his serve, **(b)** the current server returns the ball after just serving it, or **(c)** the current server misses the ball on the return.

When any of these happen, it's the other player or team's turn to serve.

⑤ Deciding the winner

The first person or team to make it to twenty-one points is the winner!

EXPERT STRATEGIES

Handball domination doesn't come easy. But the following handy tips will help you handily defeat a handful of opponents.

Playing Some Mean "D"

Because only the server can score during a game of hand-ball, playing some serious defense is sometimes the only way to stay in the game when you're not serving. While keeping an eye on the server and watching her moves helps, having solid defense skills and some catlike mobility can help you turn the tables.

Assume the Position

Posture is everything, and the best way to stand when on defense is in a straddle stance—your feet are spread a little further than a shoulder's length apart. Keep your knees bent, your hips loose, and try to keep your weight on the balls of your feet. This will make it easier to move at a moment's notice.

Sweep Side to Side

The best way to move about is by sweeping one leg over to the other and moving in side-to-side motions. This will help you keep you focus on the wall and the movements on the ball while still being able to briskly move about.

Mind your Hands

Hey, this is Handball, right? So make sure your hands are still the stars of the show. Keep them up and ready, hovering just around waist height. This will put them in ready position that allows you to quickly move them up and down when needed.

FUN FACT

The roots of racquetball reach back to one man from Connecticut: Joseph Sobek. In the 1940s, this former tennis pro wanted to create an indoor sport that was less hard on his hands than handball. So he created a new game that needed a new kind of ball. He worked for years to create just the right ball. And now, kids are using it for a playground version of handball again.

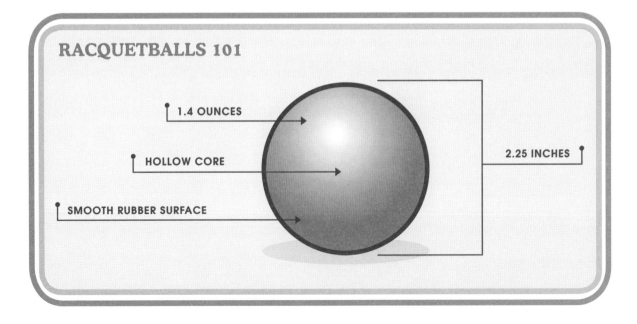

RACQUETBALLS 101

1.4 OUNCES

HOLLOW CORE

SMOOTH RUBBER SURFACE

2.25 INCHES

OTHER WAYS TO PLAY
Swedish

Swedish, which is suspected to have originated in the New England states where it was most often enjoyed, shares a lot of similarities with Handball. Like Handball, players begin by throwing the ball at the wall and waiting for it to bounce off and return back. The difference, however, is that players are tasked with doing a predetermined list of actions before hitting the ball back to the wall on its return.

For instance, after the first bounce, players would count "one," and hit the ball back to the wall. When the ball returns, players would count "two," and clap twice before smacking the ball back to the wall. When it returns again, the players would count "three," and hit the ball with the heel of their fists. This would continue, with players hitting the ball in a different, predetermined way on each count with the goal of making it to ten. If a player missed the ball or messed up, it would be the next player's turn, with each player trying to make it to the number ten.

BUTTBALL
The Thrill of Victory Meets the Agony of Getting Hit in the Backside

WHAT IT IS
Both celebrated and feared on recess yards around the world, Buttball is responsible for some of the greatest triumphs as well as some of the sorest butts. This is a game of skill, speed, and cunning that forces players to think on their feet and outplay their opponents—or otherwise subject themselves (and their backsides) to the mercy of others. Much like Patball, the game is played with nothing more than a wall, a ball, a group of players, and some courage.

WHAT'S THE POINT?
The official object of the game is to be the last player remaining in the game after all other players are eliminated—after committing "outs." The unofficial object of the game is to inflict pain on the backsides of your opponents. Buttball can be played endlessly (until the bell rings) or by the "Three Strikes and You're Out" rule.

HOW YOU PLAY
1 The opening chuck
All players line up about 20 feet from the wall. The player who brought the ball—or who won Firsts—starts the game off by bouncing the ball against the wall without letting the ball hit the ground. After the ball bounces off the wall, players must let the ball bounce off the floor once before trying to catch it.

2 Bounce back
Any player other than the one who just threw it must catch the ball after it bounces off the wall and the ground, then immediately throw it back at the wall. Fielding it cleanly means: **(a)** you catch the ball after one bounce on the pavement, **(b)** you catch it with one hand, **(c)** you don't drop the ball or have it touch another body part, and **(d)** you throw it back against to the wall without letting it bounce on the ground.

Game Stats

STYLE: Throw and catch game
PLAYERS: Three to ten (though more can play if you have enough room)
REQUIREMENTS:
A wall
A racquetball
SKILLS:
Great aim
High pain tolerance
Fast feet
Good catching and throwing ability

- - - - - - - - - -

ALSO KNOWN AS
Suicide (or "Suey")
Red Butt
Burn Ball
Peg Ball
Slaughterhouse ·
Off the Wall
Wall Ball
Butts Up
Rump Rounders
Stitch
Bear Trap
Fumble
Stinger
Fire in the Bum

③ Earning your outs

If a player mishandles the ball and the ball touches the ground, they must try to touch the wall before another player fields and throws the ball against the wall.

Depending on the pre-agreed on rules, fouls can include:

- Dropping the ball
- Getting hit with the ball as it comes off the wall
- Missing the wall during the throwback
- Bouncing the ball before it hits the wall
- Using two hands to catch the ball
- Hitting the penalized player in the head during Butts Up
- Missing the penalized player during Butts Up
- If you catch the ball right after you threw it
- Being the closest to the ball if it bounces on the ground more than once
- Taking more than two steps with a caught ball before throwing it

④ Hitting the wall

Once the foul is committed, the player must "hit the wall"—run and touch the wall before another player can throw the ball at said wall. There are three potential outcomes: **(a)** the player touches the wall before the ball does, and play continues, **(b)** the ball beats the player to the wall and the player receives an out, and **(c)** the ball hits the player on the way to the wall, and the player also receives an out.

⑤ Butt, meet ball

When a player collects three outs, he has to stand at the wall and go "Butts Up." With his palms on the wall and his butt sticking out, all other players get one shot to throw the ball as hard as they want at the player's butt. Once everyone gets a turn to peg the player with the ball, the game continues on as before.

Coach Says . . .

We prefer the simplicity of three outs—it also increases the chance of someone getting beaned during a twenty-minute recess break.

OPTIONAL RULES

Like many recess games, Buttball has been spread all over the country by kids who bring the game from one recess yard to another. Sometimes when this happens, the rules have been changed a little bit depending on where you're playing. Here's a list of some common additional rules you may find if you play Buttball on different recess yards.

Savies

This rule allows a player to ask for help from another player if he thinks he's too far to hit the wall with the ball. When a player calls "savies" he can throw the ball to another player and then go and touch the wall. If the other player wants, they can wait until the player tags the wall, or they can stab them in the back and try to throw them out.

Stripping

A player can attempt to strip the ball from the hand of another player. If he does, both he and the player who lost the ball must run to the wall to avoid being thrown out by another player.

Poison

When someone catches the ball without the ball hitting the ground, they say "poison." Now the thrower of that ball is the "poisoned" person and they must run to the wall before the person who caught the ball throws it to the wall.

SAFETY PATROL: A standard racquetball is the preferred choice for Buttball. It's lightweight and will be less painful on impact than other small game balls.

PEGGING TECHNIQUES

Let's face it: one of the best parts of Buttball is being able to peg someone in the rear with a racquetball.

Get a Grip

On the ball, that is. Make sure your hands are dry and your thumb, index, and middle fingers are all wrapped around the ball properly. This will help control your aim.

Aim Low

It's called Buttball for a reason. Hitting a player in the head is an instant out. Hitting them in the back or legs may sting them, but won't be nearly as funny. When it's time to take a penalty shot, make sure you're aiming for the bottom and nothing else.

Don't Throw Too Hard

The harder you throw, the less control you have. The less control you have, the poorer your aim will be, and the more likely you'll completely miss. Try to find a balance between speed, control, and velocity.

Have Mercy

It may soon be you standing at the wall while the other players take target practice with your butt. Earn some good karma by throwing the ball super soft or purposely missing altogether. The player at the wall may remember it later.

RECEIVING TECHNIQUES

Even though the other players are aiming at your butt, they may miss and strike other less-padded body parts. Stand in this optimal position to protect your sensitive places and minimize pain.

Assume the Position

It's important to be in the right position to receive your penalty shot to the rear.

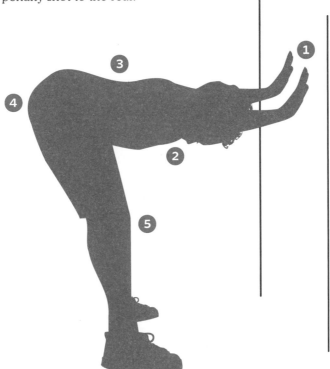

1 Hands: put your palms flat against the wall, a little less than shoulder-width apart. Keeping them this distance will hide them behind your shoulders and protect them.

2 Head: even though it's off limits, accidents do happen. Tuck you chin into your chest and keep your head as low as you can.

3 Back: keep your back rounded inward to better distribute the force if it gets hit.

4 Butt: stick it out proudly. The butt is one of the most padded parts of your body and it can take some hits. Stick it out and give them a good target.

5 Legs: keep them spread apart, knees slightly bent and loose. If you're lucky, the ball may sail right between your legs.

Prepare What You Wear

It's not always an option during the hot and humid summer, but a pair of jeans or corduroys can help give some extra padding and protection. Also, baggier is always better—the extra material can absorb some of the force of the ball.

Never, Ever, Turn Around

Going Butts Up is not unlike going in front of a firing squad—the anticipation alone can be monumental. But never give in and turn around. Not only will it make you more nervous, you could get hit in the face with an errant shot.

Stay Relaxed . . . If Possible

Speaking of staying relaxed, keeping yourself limp and loose can make a big difference when getting nailed with incoming rubber balls. While it may seem like a good idea to tense up like a wall, doing this can actually increase the amount of pain you'll feel. Try to think happy thoughts while staying calm and relaxed.

OTHER WAYS TO PLAY
Butt Dodgeball

This variation combines the thrill of Buttball with the skill of Dodgeball. One player is the thrower while all the other players, called dodgers, line up with their back against the wall. The thrower chucks the ball at each player, trying to peg them with it. If a dodger gets hit, he's then the thrower. The dodgers are only allowed to move left and right; if they move away from the wall at all, it's Butts Up time and thrower gets to take a penalty shot. The game is endless and goes on until everyone decides to call it a day.

PATBALL
Buttball's Orderly British Cousin

WHAT IT IS

In the United Kingdom kids have been playing Patball for decades. Patball is like a lot of other wall games in that it involves smacking (not throwing) a ball at the wall. What makes it different is that a player must hit the ball to the floor so that it bounces from the floor to the wall, and then bounces from there back to the players. This extra bounce means that players have to add a little skill and strength to each pat of the ball.

On top of that, players have to hit the ball in a certain order, meaning patience and willpower are the keys to winning. Because there can be a ton of players going at it at once, the real trick to Patball is making sure you know who's turn it is and when. Fast, furious, and intense, Patball is not for those who daydream through recess time.

WHAT'S THE POINT?

While there are a lot of ways to play Patball, the main goal is always the same: bounce the ball off the wall in just the right way so that the next player in line is unable to do the same. When a player can't hit or bounce the ball right, he's out. The last player standing wins the game!

Game Stats

STYLE: Throw and catch game
PLAYERS: Two or more
REQUIREMENTS:
A tennis ball (or rubber ball)
A wall (one big enough to support all the players)
SKILLS:
Strong hands
A thick skull
Patience
Discipline
Fast feet
Steel nerves

Learning the Lingo

While terms like "obs" and "curbs" (or "kerbs") may sound odd, they're pretty important rules for the game, just like the following terms:

DRAG (A.K.A. VOLLEY): occurs when a player scoops the ball up instead of patting it.

DOUBLE BOUNCE SCOOP-UPS: the player lets the ball bounce more than once before hitting it.

BLIND: the act of getting in front of another player, so he can't see the ball.

DIRECT (A.K.A. STRAIGHT ENDS): patting the ball to the wall without bouncing it on the ground first.

SELF-OBS (A.K.A. SPIKE OR BODY BITS): this is called when the ball accidentally hits a player after bouncing on the wall.

KILLER: a serve that can't be played and needs to be re-served.

CONDITIONAL: called when something messes up the game and it's nobody's fault.

MOUNTAINS: when the ball bounces off the wall and flies high.

BELOW-KNEES: a low-bouncing ball.

WORMBURNER: a ball that bounces so low it hugs the ground.

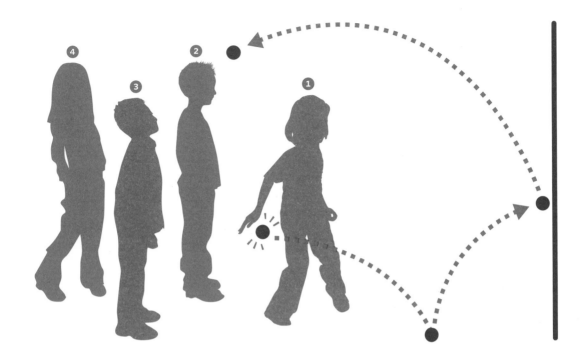

HOW YOU PLAY

1 Pick the order

The player who brought the ball gets to decide the order by assigning each player a number, or the order can be arranged by the order players arrived in. This will determine who gets to hit the ball and in which order.

2 The big bounce

Patball begins with player one patting the ball to the ground so that it bounces up and still hits the wall hard enough to bounce back.

3 The return

As the ball bounces back, it's up to player two to move in. He pats the ball back to the floor so it bounces back to the wall. Then it's player three's turn to do the same thing.

4 Take turns

This process continues as each player pats the ball to the wall and the next player follows, doing the same thing. Once the last player pats the ball, it's player one's turn again.

⑤ Next round

Players keep taking turns patting the ball. If a player misses his turn or messes up the bounce, he's out. Once a player is out, a new round starts with player one serving the ball. This keeps going until there are only two players left.

⑥ Showdown

When it's down to only two players, the game goes into showdown mode. The rules are the same, but the remaining players engage in a best-of-three match. The first player to get his opponent out twice wins the game.

ADDITIONAL RULES

- You can only pat the ball when it's your turn. If you go out of turn, you're out.

- You can only pat the ball with your hand and your head. No catching, scooping, or throwing. Kicking may be allowed, depending on who you're playing with.

- Whenever a player serves, the ball must hit the ground once and only once before hitting the wall.

- After the ball bounces from the wall, players are allowed to let the ball bounce on the ground once, or they can go for it and pat the ball out of the air.

- If the ball hits something or someone before the next player has a chance to hit it, that player can call "obs," which means the round starts over with the player that called obs serving. Everyone playing has to agree to allow calling obs before the start of the game.

- If the ball bounces wild because it hit a weird or uneven part of the wall, a player can call "curbs" or a "dodgy bounce." If everyone agrees, then a rethrow can be allowed.

- If a player doesn't like the serve the player before him threw, he can call for a re-serve. He can only do this once per game.

- The demon rule states that a player who is out can play "demon" and hangout in front of the wall to catch any shot other than the serve. If the demon can catch the ball before it hits the wall, he replaces the player who threw it and that player is out. If the demon can't catch the ball and he gets hit with it, it's an obs. If the ball obs twice, the demon is out of the game for good.

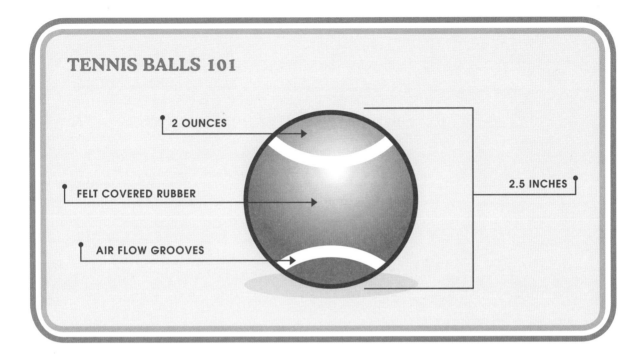

TENNIS BALLS 101

2 OUNCES

FELT COVERED RUBBER

AIR FLOW GROOVES

2.5 INCHES

EXPERT STRATEGIES

Professional Patballers know that a victory should not be decided on just the bounce of a ball. Here are three secret strategies that will help you step up your game.

Pick the Weakest Link

If you have any say in which number in the order you're assigned, make sure you're the number right before the worst player in the game. This means an easy out for them and one less challenger for you.

Aim Low and Hard

If a player attempts to go after the ball and can't get it, they're out. So make sure you bounce the ball in a way that will make it difficult enough for the next player to miss while still being a fair enough ball to not invite a rethrow. The best way to do this is to pat the ball low and hard, so that it bounces against the wall at just above knee-height. This will keep the ball in fair play while making it extremely difficult for your opponents to connect.

Headbutt

Using your head for Patball looks incredibly cool, especially if you do it right! To pull this off, wait for a high-bouncing ball, when it gets close, use the pointy part of your head (the part just above the center of your forehead) to pop the ball back at the wall.

OTHER WAYS TO PLAY

Aces

Aces is played with exactly four players on a grid of eight squares of equal measurement that is painted, taped, or chalked on the ground to make the court. Each player is stuck in their own single square, and instead of using a wall, you're bouncing the ball off the other squares on the court.

Each player starts with three lives. After each out, a player loses a life. Once a player is out of lives, she becomes a ghost, which means she can play but she can't get anybody else out. When it's down to two players, the showdown rules are the same as in regular Patball, but instead, each player gets control of four of the eight squares, which they must stay in at all times.

Kingpin

Kingpin is played with three to eight players on a painted, taped, or chalked court instead of a wall, just like Aces. What's different is that instead of being player one, player two, and so on, each player is called King, Queen, first Jack, second Jack, third Jack, and so on. The first person to lose the round gets the worst rank, the second person out gets the second worst rank, and so on. The winner is named King. When the next round starts, everyone has their titles and the goal is to stay in the game long enough to earn a higher rank.

Wall Ball

Very similar to traditional Patball, Wall Ball is played almost the same way, but without the ordered players. In other words, it's a free for all with any player going for the ball whenever they feel like it. Instead of outs, each player gets a strike anytime she messes up, and three strikes means she is out of the game. This variation also eliminates the showdown portion of Patball, meaning the last man standing is the winner.

TETHERBALL
The Skill of Volleyball Meets the Speed of Formula 1

WHAT IT IS

A standard on North American playgrounds, Tetherball is a study of contractions. It's fast-paced but requires very little running. A ball is hit, smashed and clobbered—but never goes out of bounds. Half of its equipment can be created from household materials, but the other half need to be professionally manufactured. In some sense, the name itself represents these two sides of the game. The "ball," the ultimate symbol of freedom and play, is connected literally by the "tether," the opposite force that keeps it contained and trapped.

WHAT'S THE POINT?

The game is a classic battle for territory—but vertical, and twisted. A player wins by causing the rope to wind completely around the pole in his desired direction.

Game Stats

STYLE: Reaction game
PLAYERS: Two
REQUIREMENTS:
A tetherball
Tether pole
SKILLS:
Hand-eye coordination
Upper body strength

TETHERBALL EQUIPMENT 101

POLE
1.5–2 inches in diameter
8–10 feet
Swivel hook
Nylon tether cord

BALL
24–26 inch circumference
Weighs 13–16 oz.
Nylon or soft rubber
Internal cord connector

10 FEET

2 FEET

The History of Tetherball

Back in the late 1800s, tennis was the toast of Europe as it had only recently evolved to an outdoor game—it was actually called "lawn tennis" to separate it from "real tennis" which was an indoor sport for royalty. With tennis fever taking over the land, a new game was invented to solve the problem of needing full tennis courts and friends to help chase down balls.

This early version of Tetherball was basically a tennis ball on a rope attached to a pole smacked at high speeds with tennis racquets. This new, fast-paced game quickly became the talk of town. In fact, an article included in an 1899 edition of *The New York Times* reported that tetherball was "making its way at the fashionable resorts and bids fair to check the growing popularity of the old favorite croquet, and also of tennis."

The only thing missing was interest from kids, but that changed in 1948 when the Voit Rubber company—those geniuses who invented both the playground ball and the beach ball—devised a version of Tetherball that used a larger ball and no racquets. This slower, more smackable version was easier to pick and became hugely popular. So adults left the game and kids took over—with popularity reaching its peak in the 1970s and 1980s. Unfortunately, by the 1990's Tetherball's popularity cooled, and it was but a punchline in the movie *Napoleon Dynamite*.

But as Tetherball has taught us: What goes around, comes around. And today, there appears to be something of a Tetherball resurgence. Kids and adults are rediscovering the game, making their own poles, and getting back to hitting. So, in other words: Game's back on!

HOW YOU PLAY

❶ Side or direction

After deciding Firsts, the first player gets to pick the side or direction they want to move the ball in. This can be advantageous since the player can choose the direction that suits their dominant hand—or the player can chose the side and position that forces their opponent to face the sun. Since the game often requires one to look skyward, being forced look toward the blinding light of our closest star can be a decided disadvantage.

❷ Serve up the serve

Unlike other games, a server in Tetherball has an immediate advantage since they can quickly pull off a victory spiral—a series of single-direction hits that finishes off an opponent. To accomplish this and level the playground playing field, the opponent must hit the ball once before the server can touch it again.

❸ Volley

Each player will continue to hit the ball in their designated direction. The volleys back-and-forth can continue indefinitely as long as nobody commits a foul.

❹ The tether fouls

When a player commits one of the following violations, the play stops and the ball goes to their opponent. The fouls include:

- Hitting the ball with any part of the body other than the hands
- Touching the ball twice before a full rotation
- Holding or catching the ball during play
- Touching the pole with any part of your body
- Hitting or catching the rope
- Stepping inside the neutral zone (see diagram on page 189)

❺ That's a wrap

The winner is the first person to wrap the ball all the way in their direction with the two following requirements: **(a)** the entire length of rope needs to wind around the pole to the point that the spin is stopped by the ball, and **(b)** the ball must hit the pole above the scoring line—usually above the 5-foot mark.

SAFETY PATROL: This game can get fast paced so beware of the whereabouts of the ball—you could get hit by the ball as it whips around, or get tangled in the rope. Stay sharp!

WORLD OF PLAY

Take Swingball and lose the pole and rope, and you have "Raketa," a Greek game where players hit a tennis ball back and forth, trying not to drop the ball and ruin the rally.

⑥ Best of . . .

If only two people are playing, it is recommended to play a best-of-five series. If three to five people are playing, a best-of-three series is easier. If over five people are playing with one pole, a one-and-done structure will allow everyone to join the fun. The ball is served into play, but without the requirement for a first touch from the receiver.

OPTIONAL RULES

Full Body Hit

Rather than penalize a player for touching the ball with any body part other than the hand, this rule encourages players to use any and all body parts.

Pole Serve

Another way to even out the server's advantage, this rule states that the server must bounce the ball off the pole before hitting it.

Pole Drop

When both players commit simultaneous fouls, play is restarted by each player putting one hand on the ball, and releasing it. After the ball hits the pole, either player is allowed to go after it.

Tot Tether

The rule of having to have the ball wrap above the 5-foot mark is waived for when children play.

HITTING TECHNIQUES

The Punch

While the ball may recall a boxing speed bag, resist the temptation to closed-fist punch the ball. Instead strike at the ball with the meaty part of your hand. This technique offers more control, but less power.

The Slap

This open-handed technique gives you more control, but a bit less power. It works in both single-handed and double-handed varieties.

EXPERT STRATEGIES

While it may seem circular, there is plenty of room for strategy. As anyone who has played the game knows: brute force alone won't win the game.

Orbit of Awesome

The goal is simple: Keep the ball out of your opponent's reach. Do this by hitting the ball as high and vertical as possible. Ideally, this angled hit will be too high for them to get, making winning as simple as just keeping the ball moving as consistently as possible.

Jamming Block

In an ideal world, each player is slugging the ball back and forth in an elegant rhythm. In reality, the game is more aggressive and once one player starts to dominate, a jamming block is required to stop the run. This is accomplished by jumping up and using your fist to interrupt the spin, even if it is at the expense of ball control.

Sacrifice Spin

The seasoned player must know when to hit and when to sacrifice the hit. If the ball is coming too fast, too angled, or you simply aren't in the right position, hit the ball in your opponent's direction. This can slow down the spin to make the ball more smackable on its next go-around.

WORLD OF PLAY

In Australia, New Zealand, South Africa, and the United Kingdom, Tetherball is unknown—but they do play a similar game: Swingball. Swingball, also known as Totem Tennis, which more closely resembles the original Tetherball, is played with a smaller ball, plastic racquets, and a shorter pole.

H-O-R-S-E
A Battle of Wills, Skills, and Silly Shots

Game Stats

STYLE: Reaction game

PLAYERS: Two or more

REQUIREMENTS:

Basketball

Basketball hoop

SKILLS:

Aim

Form

Creativity

WHAT IT IS

A game of classic one-upmanship on the hard court, H-O-R-S-E clearly evolved out of its thrilling, international, billion-dollar forefather, basketball. The relation is interesting when you think about it—other than the ball and the hoop, the two games have very little in common. H-O-R-S-E is a beautiful combination of creativity and competition. It also gives players who might otherwise struggle competing in a full basketball game a chance to join the fun and enjoy the camaraderie and the innocent delights of the granny shot.

WHAT'S THE POINT?

The game is in the name. The goal is to avoid getting five penalties—indicated by each letter of the word "H-O-R-S-E." When you get all five penalties, you're out. The last player standing wins. Of course, the fun of the game lies not just in making shots—it's about making shots while being as creative, athletic, and devious as possible.

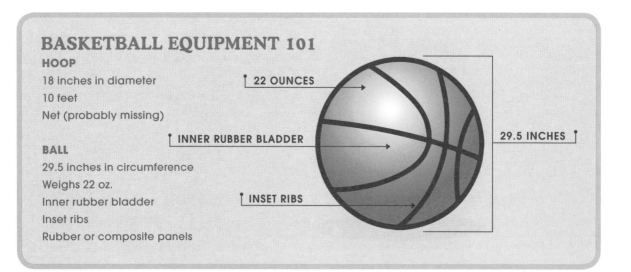

BASKETBALL EQUIPMENT 101

HOOP

18 inches in diameter

10 feet

Net (probably missing)

BALL

29.5 inches in circumference

Weighs 22 oz.

Inner rubber bladder

Inset ribs

Rubber or composite panels

22 OUNCES

INNER RUBBER BLADDER

29.5 INCHES

INSET RIBS

HOW YOU PLAY

1 Take a shot, any shot

After deciding Firsts, the game starts when the first player takes a shot. It is important that the player creating the shot first explains it. For example, the shooter will say, "Left hand, one foot behind the free-throw line." This ensures that the player is intentionally making the shot, not just making the shot out of pure luck. Half the fun of H-O-R-S-E is being creative, so tricky shots are encouraged.

2 Follow the leader

If the shooter makes the shot, the next player must replicate that same exact shot in the same exact way: the stance, positioning, and placement all have to look exactly as it did when the first player took the shot.

- If there are only two players involved, the first shooter will remain in control, as the player who goes first continues to invent shots until she misses one, at which point the other player gets the chance to attempt a shot of his own choosing.

- If there are more than two players, it is recommended that the next player up in the order automatically gets to take the first shot after a round.

3 Getting the letter

If a player is unable to duplicate a shot—if the ball does not go in, or the technique is not identical—that player is assigned a penalty in the form of a letter. The first penalty assigned is an "H," the second is an "O," the third is an "R," and so on. A player cannot get a letter when missing a shot of his own invention—only when trying to duplicate another player's shot.

4 Last one standing

Game play continues until all but one player has been eliminated. If there is a time limitation, like the recess bell ringing, the player with the fewest letters is deemed the winner.

FUN FACT

Basketball was invented in 1891 and was originally played with soccer balls, which were impossible to dribble.

Coach Says . . .

Distracting a player from her shot is not good form. This is not some heathen game like golf, it's a game of class.

FUN FACT

Indoor basketballs are traditionally made with leather, which would be destroyed by the rough surface of concrete courts.

OPTIONAL RULES

No Repeats

A shot style cannot be used twice. Once a shot is made, it is retired from that round.

Proving the Shot

After someone gets H-O-R-S-E, the person who originally made the last shot must make the shot again to prove that the shot was made because of skill, not due to luck. If that player can't make it again, the player who was going to be out loses the "E" and stays in the game.

Tipping (a.k.a. Tip-Horse)

This rule adds insult to injury. After a shooter misses, the following player can attempt to tip in the ball before it falls to the ground. If he can, the shooter who missed gets two letters, not just one.

OTHER WAYS TO PLAY

P-I-G (a.k.a. O-U-T)

If time is of the essence and the school bell is about to ring, a shorter three-out version is perfect. Players count three misses with the words P-I-G, or with the less metaphorically consistent, O-U-T.

H-O-R-S-E Extreme

If there are props available, bring them into the game as well. Blindfolds, trampolines, skateboards, whatever you can get your hands on. Make the most of the space you have and go wild with creating tricky shots around outrageous obstacles.

Other Basketball-Based Games

Over the past century or so, basketball has taken the world (and its playgrounds) by storm. Here are several other games that involve putting the ball through the hoop in various ways.

FIVES

This game is a faster-paced, potentially less inventive version of H-O-R-S-E. Two or more players line up along the top of the key. The first player takes a shot. If she makes it, she doesn't get any points and the next player gets the ball. If she doesn't make it, she must rebound her shot and take another one from that exact place. She continues until she makes a basket—a maximum of five shots. If she doesn't, she receives a point. The following player must now attempt to make a basket in the same or fewer shots. If he can't, he too receives a point. Players are eliminated when they reach five points, and the last player standing wins.

AROUND THE WORLD
(A.K.A. AROUND THE KEY)

This multiplayer game involves a sequence of shooting positions. The most common are the seven positions that are marked along the key of the court (the painted box that extends from under the basket toward the foul line, see illustration). Each player takes turns attempting to shoot from each of the positions. If a player misses, he can either start from that last position on his next turn, or he can take a chance shot. If the chance shot goes in he can keep possession and move on. If he misses, however, he must start from the first position at his next turn. The first player to make a basket from each of the positions wins.

LIGHTNING (A.K.A. KNOCKOUT)

This game uses two balls to add more competition to the mix. The first two players line up at the top of the key with their balls. The first player takes his shot. If he makes the shot, he tosses the ball to the third player in line and returns to the back of the line. If he misses, he must immediately try to rebound and score. While this is happening, the second player attempts to make her shot the moment the ball first leaves the hands of the first player. The second player's goal is to make her shot first, which would eliminate the first player. This pattern continues as a new player steps up from the line and ends when only one player is left. The spoils for the winner of the previous round is to be able pick the spot and order of the subsequent round.

Insider Secrets:
H-O-R-S-E with the Skills

Are you planning on showing up opponents and showing off to friends on the H-O-R-S-E court? Then you better have the kind of skills that pay the bills. According to Chris Spatola, former Duke University Men's Basketball assistant coach and current college hoops TV analyst, the key to H-O-R-S-E comes down to one, actually two, things: sturdy legs.

"Legs are the foundation of your shot," says Spatola. "If you're not on balance you won't have an accurate release." Once you have your balance, Spatola suggests locking your shooting arm's elbow to keep your aim straight, bending your knees to put some power behind the ball and pushing the shot through nice and easy in one flowing motion. "Holding your follow-through ensures you are repeating the same motion on every shot," he says.

Now that you have the form down, which shots should you go for? Spatola has a few go-to favorites to help add letters to his opponent's card, such as the weak hand shot—a shot taken anywhere using the opponent's nondominant hand—and "the behind the backboard" shot. "This is the Bermuda Triangle of H-O-R-S-E shots," he says of the shot, which calls for using a high arc to get the ball to land at the top of the backboard and fall into the basket.

If you're looking for quick results, nothing makes a H-O-R-S-E out of your opponent faster than the classic half-court shot. "A lot of H-O-R-S-E traditionalists loathe this shot," he says, "but the fact is, if you do make this, it's a guaranteed letter for your opponent."

Chris Spatola is a former Duke University Men's Basketball assistant coach and current college hoops TV analyst on the CBS Sports and PAC-12 Networks. For more information visit ChrisSpatola.com

Insider Secrets:
H-O-R-S-E by the Numbers

In H-O-R-S-E, you have a whole court full of spots to sink shots from, allowing you to potentially beat—and, if you're lucky, embarrass—your opponent. But which do you choose?

This was the conundrum Ben Blatt—former member of Harvard Sports Analysis Collective—ran into while growing up on the rough side of the court. But as they say, when the going gets tough, the tough get mathematical.

"I sought to find the best way to win at H-O-R-S-E according to statistical theory. Some people might suggest practicing my jump shot if I truly wanted to win, but I was playing to my strength," says Blatt, whose strength was clearly statistics. Blatt realized that while trick shots look awesome, they're tough for all players to make, not just the opponent. And while lay-ups may seem like a slam dunk (pardon our pun), they're so easy that the opposition will have no problem making it.

Realizing this, Blatt came up with a plan to figure out the most statistically sound way to make a H-O-R-S-E out of his opponents—by burying them with their inability to make common shots. "Imagine you take a behind-the-back-eyes-closed-swish shot that you figure has a 10 percent chance of going in. Ten times out of 100 the shot will go in and of those ten times, only once would you expect your opponent to make the shot. This would mean you would give your opponent a letter 9 percent of the time," Blatt explains. "Or, imagine you take a shot from six feet away that goes in 80 percent of the time. Eighty times out of one hundred your shot would go in and you can expect your opponent to make it sixty-four of these times. You'd give your opponent a letter 16 percent of the time."

In other words, unless your opponent has the name "Kobe" on his driver's license, there's more opportunity for you to crush him by making average shots than there is of you nailing him with unruly trick shots.

Ben Blatt is a former member of Harvard Sports Analysis Collective and current Slate *staff writer as well as coauthor of* I Don't Care If We Never Get Back. *For more information visit BBlatt.com*

TRICK SHOT TECHNIQUES

Basketball is full of form and technique, but H-O-R-S-E is a bit more creative. Rather than waste time covering the basics, here are several of the trickier shots.

The Granny

This is a throwback shot that involves throwing the ball up with both hands from between your legs. Spread your feet a little more than shoulder-width apart, place your hands underneath the ball, and hold it at about thigh level. Then throw the ball upward toward the hoop.

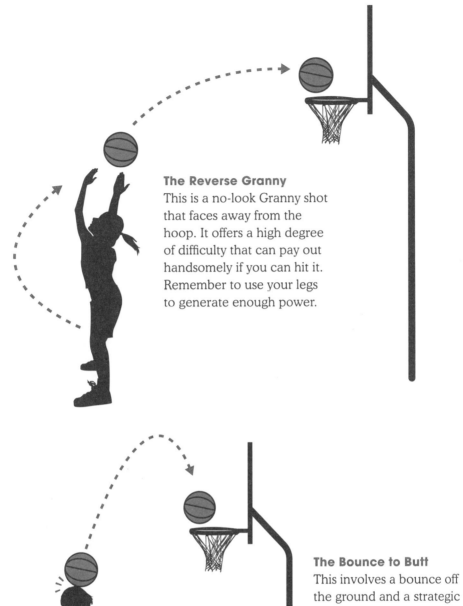

The Reverse Granny
This is a no-look Granny shot that faces away from the hoop. It offers a high degree of difficulty that can pay out handsomely if you can hit it. Remember to use your legs to generate enough power.

The Bounce to Butt
This involves a bounce off the ground and a strategic head-butt of the ball into the hoop. Be warned, this will hurt, but if you use the hardest part of your head (the pointy part at the top of your forehead) you should be able to get enough bounce to get it in the net.

5 FIFTH PERIOD

CONTACT SPORTS

Subtlety, Grace, Gentleness . . . Not Here

Men should learn to live with the same seriousness with which children play.
— **Nietzsche**

Human contact is essential to our lives. When you make that contact at a full-out sprint on the blacktop—it's even better. Contact games fill a primal need that is lacking in our culture. They fill that need we all have to reach out and touch someone—sometimes by whizzing a ball at their heads. So it's time we turn our attention to this category of games that really touch everyone.

DODGEBALL
A Fast-Paced Game of No-Holds-Barred Awesomeness

Game Stats

STYLE: Throw and catch game

PLAYERS: Six per team, the more the merrier

REQUIREMENTS:

Six rubber dodgeballs

Court

SKILLS:

Hand-eye coordination

Speedy reflexes

Agility

Aim

Throwing

SAFETY PATROL: Make sure you use a ball designed specifically for Dodgeball, other types of balls may be too heavy or dangerous and can cause some damage.

WHAT IT IS

Dodgeball is one of the most celebrated and most controversial games in the history of the blacktop. For its fans, it's a thrilling fast-paced sport that demands agility, speed, accuracy, and keen strategy. For its detractors, it's a barbaric survival of the fittest game that must be banned from all schools, playgroups, and camps. The truth is that the game is what you make of it. And when played correctly with a healthy sense of competition, few games can match this iconic activity.

WHAT'S THE POINT?

Avoid getting hit while eliminating players on the other team by hitting them with a ball or catching a ball thrown by the opposing team.

HOW YOU PLAY

1 Set up the court

The court is divided into two 30 feet × 30 feet areas, with a 4 feet × 30 feet neutral zone located at center court separating the two sides. There is also an attack line located parallel and 10 feet from the center line, for a total court length of 60 feet from end line to end line, and a total width of 30 feet from sideline to sideline.

Approximately 2–3 feet should be allotted for an out-of-bounds area—an unobstructed space around the outside of all the boundaries.

Every effort should be made to obtain the correct dimensions, however court size may be adjusted to best suit the available space.

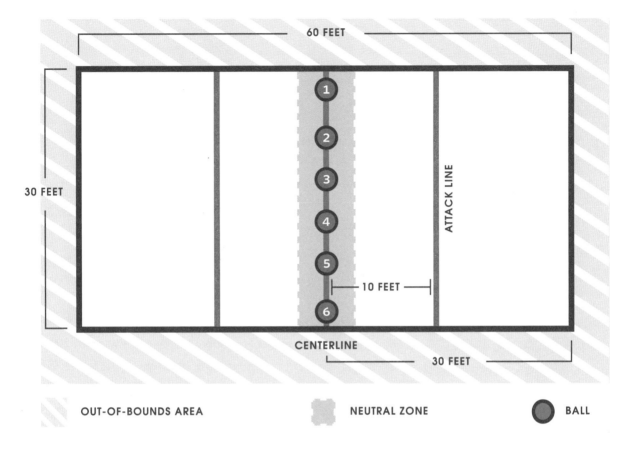

60 FEET

30 FEET

ATTACK LINE

10 FEET

CENTERLINE

30 FEET

OUT-OF-BOUNDS AREA   NEUTRAL ZONE   BALL

② Choose your weapon

There are two types of balls that are approved for Dodgeball, **(a)** a traditional 8.5-inch inflatable playground ball, and **(b)** a 8-inch low-impact foam core ball.

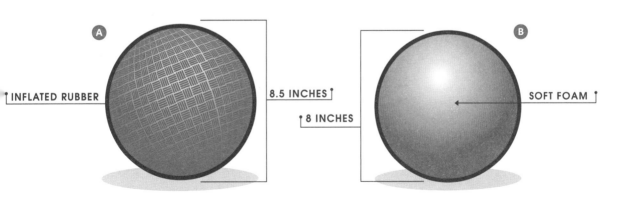

INFLATED RUBBER   8.5 INCHES   8 INCHES   SOFT FOAM

To keep the game moving, you should designate players as retrievers so you don't lose precious pegging time chasing after stray out-of-bounds balls. Retrievers can be either players who are out or waiting to jump in the next game.

When you're ready to play, line up six balls on the center line spanning the width of the court.

❸ Pick your players

Pick teams using one of the methods listed on page 18. Teams consist of six players per team.

❹ The rush

Play begins with all players positioned anywhere behind their team's end line. The rush occurs at the beginning of each game or reset—upon an official signal, both teams rush to center court and attempt to retrieve as many balls as possible. A team may rush with as many or as few players as it wants, but at least one person from each team has to rush. There is no limit to how many balls an individual player may retrieve.

❺ Putting a ball in play

The player and the ball must return completely behind the attack line. During the rush, any ball retrieved from the neutral zone must be returned behind the attack line before it may be thrown at an opponent. A ball that hasn't crossed the attack line is considered a dead ball, and any hits or catches are voided plays.

SAFETY PATROL: Don't throw at someone's head. It's not cool or safe. There is plenty of the body to aim for. And much less risk of injury.

A ball can be put into play following a rush when: **(a)** a player carries the ball across the attack line, **(b)** a player passes the ball to a teammate who is behind or carries it across the attack line, or **(c)** a player rebounds the ball off the back wall of a closed court.

Coach Says . . .

Momentum may carry a player out of bounds while making a catch. But if control of the ball was established before going out of bounds, the player is "safe."

6 Outs

Out players must stand behind their own end line, outside of the out-of-bounds area where they can either stand around and nurse their wounds or serve as retrievers for their team. Following are the four ways that constitute a player being declared out: **(a)** when a live ball hits any part of the player's body or clothing, **(b)** when a player is hit by a live ball that rebounded off another player or ball, **(c)** when an opposing player catches the live ball they just threw to the opposing side, or **(d)** if any part of the player's body touches the sidelines, end lines, or neutral zone line.

7 Blocking

Players can defend themselves by blocking the ball in flight with a ball they are holding, as long as they retain control of the ball they are using to block. If a player drops or loses possession of the blocking ball, they are out.

Any blocked ball rebounding off another ball is considered live. Any player hit by the rebounding ball is deemed out.

8 Freeing players

When a player makes a catch, an out player from their team can return from the sidelines back into play. Players return in the order they were put out (i.e., first out, first in).

9 Winning

There are three main game types with different ways to win each. Make sure everyone agrees on which game type you are playing prior to the rush.

A **ELIMINATION GAME:** The most common game that is played until all opponents on one side have been eliminated. The first team to eliminate all of its opponents is declared the winner.

B **TIMED GAME:** A game played for a predetermined time limit, or until all opponents are eliminated on one side. If time expires, all remaining players are counted. The team with most players remaining wins the game.

C **SCORED GAME:** A scored game is played as either an elimination or timed game with points awarded not for the win, but for the number of players remaining in at the end of each game.

ADDITIONAL RULES
The Neutral Zone

The neutral zone is the 4 feet × 30 feet area centered on the center line. A player may safely step into the neutral zone on either side of the center line but crossing the zone results in a foul.

- Any player crossing over the neutral zone into their opponents' side of the court will be called out

- Players may not slide or dive head first into the neutral zone or they will be called out

- Players may not physically pull another player across the neutral zone or prevent them from returning to their side of the court

Coach Says . . .

There is no stalling allowed in Dodgeball. All players must throw their ball within five seconds of gaining possession. If you stall, the other players are allowed to call "stall" and the stalling player's entire team loses possession of all their balls. It's not worth it to stall—keep the game moving, people!

Insider Secrets: Dodgeball Skills

On the surface, Dodgeball seems as simple as chucking rubber balls at your opponent, but to seasoned pros like Ed Prentiss, founder of the National Dodgeball League and the Dodgeball World Championships, there's much more to the game than simply throw, dodge, repeat.

OFFENSE

Prentiss recommends trying out different throwing styles to see what fits best for you. Just as important as mastering your throw is timing it to sync with your teammates. "The most important strategy on offense is to throw together," he suggests. "It is very difficult for an opponent to react to two (or more) balls coming at them one right after another. If the team singles out an opponent and synchronizes their throws, they are much more likely to be successful."

DEFENSE

Whether you choose to dodge or catch the ball, you need to stick with the decision. "Indecision almost always results in an out," Prentiss warns. Try to anticipate the direction the balls are flying, and that commit to actively moving in that direction. And whatever you do, don't show the other team your back. "The most critical error a player can make is to turn his back, especially if the team is about to double up on him."

Secondly, while catching the ball allows you to get the thrower on the other team out immediately, it's a high-risk maneuver. To increase your chances of making a safe catch, Prentiss recommends trying to square the incoming ball with your chest and avoid reaching out to catch a ball that otherwise would fly past you. The odds you'll catch it safely are slim, and not worth the out.

PRACTICE

Prentiss recommends strengthening your weak points before facing tough competition. "If you're a great thrower, work on your catching. Some guys rely too much on throwing heat but don't survive on defense. If you're a skilled catcher or dodger work on your throwing technique. The best players are triple threats."

TEAMWORK

Try to balance your team so that everyone's strengths complement one another. "The fastest players should rush for balls and the best throwers should hang back," he suggests. "Most teams have at least one player who will be very aggressive. This player tends to play much closer to the center line and often acts as a distraction."

Ed Prentiss is the founder of the National Dodgeball League and the Dodgeball World Championships. For more information visit TheNDL.com.

DODGING TECHNIQUES

To stay in the game and avoid a stinger, you will need to avoid getting hit. Try these proven techniques to get out of the way. Hint: never hesitate and never turn your back.

Dodge

This is the workhorse of all defensive moves—and the game's namesake. Quickly move your body in the opposite direction of where the ball is traveling.

Dip

When a ball is fast approaching at waist level, turn your body to the side and pop out your hip as you watch the ball sail past your rear end. Immediately turn to face your opponents and laugh at their failed attempt.

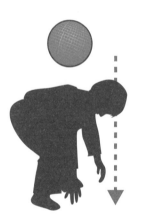

Duck

To avoid a painful head shot, simply crouch down and lower your upper body to watch the ball sail over your head. Notice that in this position you are already in the perfect stance to catch anything else that might be thrown at you.

Dive

If you get caught off guard and don't see the ball traveling at you until it's almost too late, your best option is to leap and dive to the ground to gain some extra distance in a split second. Make sure you're ready for additional balls coming at you as you try to pick yourself back up from this risky move.

THROWING TECHNIQUES

Now that you know how to avoid getting hit, you need to learn how to hit. Try these throwing techniques to see which one is right for you.

Overhand Heat

An overhand baseball throw is the most common throwing technique in Dodgeball. These typically travel the fastest and hit the hardest.

Sidearm Stinger

Sidearm throws are slower but can be difficult for players to see coming and judge their direction. Sidearm throws also allow you to put a spin on the ball that makes them harder to catch.

Underhand Whip

This throw is done with an underhanded whip action like a fast pitch softball player. When performed properly, underhand throws can be lethal because the ball is coming in unexpectedly low and fast.

OPTIONAL RULES

Add these rules to your traditional Dodgeball match to up the stakes.

Hot Ball

Players are only allowed to throw and hit an opponent who is holding a ball. A catch can occur, but the player must keep possession of both balls.

Opposite Hand

All players must throw with their nondominant hand.

Three Strikes

Each player is given three rubber bands to stretch over their forearm. Each time they are hit they must remove one rubber band. When a player runs out of rubber bands they are out of the game.

Traitors

When a player gets hit they must go and play for the other team. The game ends when all players are on one side.

OTHER WAYS TO PLAY

For an entirely new experience, try these different game play varieties to change up the fun.

Bombardment

If you are playing on a basketball court, a player can try to throw his ball at the opposing team's basket, but he must shoot it from his own half of the court. If he makes the basket (a rarity) all of his team's out players get to return to the game. Bombardment can be played with more players than the traditional six per side, and it's actually more fun to play with ten or more players per team.

Lifeguard

This version of Dodgeball employs a lifeguard, someone who can save hit players to keep the game going longer. Before the game starts, each team designates a lifeguard. Once play begins, anyone who gets hit who is not a lifeguard must sit on the floor in the spot where they were hit to wait to be rescued. While they're sitting, opponents cannot throw balls at them; anyone throwing a ball at a down player is automatically out and must leave the court. It's the lifeguard's job to duck and dodge the balls and make her way around the court, tagging seated players to get them back in the game. If the lifeguard is hit by a ball, their team loses and the game restarts.

Outsiders (a.k.a. Circle Dodgeball)
Outsiders is a version of the game played with one ball and no teams. All players, except for one (called the outsider), start inside the playing court (half of a basketball court is the perfect size, or draw a large circle similar in size). The outsider must stay outside the court and try to hit any player inside the court. Once a player is hit, they join the Outsider. The last person inside the area is the winner.

Prison Break
Similar to bombardment, but if a basketball court in unavailable you can free your "out" teammates one at a time. If a player gets out, he must go to "prison" by standing behind the opposing team's end line. To free a prisoner, teammates still in the game attempt to sneak a ball past their opponents and if a prisoner receives the ball within the designated prison area, they are free and allowed to join their remaining teammates.

Protect the President
One player from each team is chosen to be the president. The other players are soldiers and must not only battle the team by playing Dodgeball, but they must protect their president from getting hit. Once a team's president gets hit, the game is over.

Scramble
Scramble is a free-for-all with no teams. All players enter the court and one player throws the ball up into the air. The player who catches the ball becomes the attacker and tries to eliminate all the other players by hitting them with the ball below the waist. All other players are not allowed to throw. They can only dodge or catch. Any player who gets hit is eliminated and must leave the court. If a player catches a throw, the attacker is eliminated and any out players return to start a new game. The player who caught the ball is the new attacker. Any attacker who can eliminate all the other players wins.

RED ROVER
The Unforgettable and Infamous Full-Contact Classic

Game Stats

STYLE: Contact game

PLAYERS: Eight plus (ideally an even number)

REQUIREMENTS:
An open space (soft turf is best)

SKILLS:
Grip strength
Running
Taking a hit
Dusting one's self off

- - - - - - - - - - - -

ALSO KNOWN AS
Forcing the Gates
Rover

FUN FACT

Why is it called Red Rover? One theory is that it refers to pirates stealing crews as depicted in the 1829 book titled *The Red Rover*, which described these seafaring adventures.

WHAT IT IS

Red Rover is not for the faint of heart—or the fragile of body. Second only to Dodgeball in infamy, it remains one of the most loved and hated playground games. It involves a lot more brawn than brain, and because there are multiple ways to get injured it has fallen out of favor with most schools.

Red Rover has roots dating back to a nineteenth-century British game called British Bulldogs. Versions of this game are even played in other parts of the world—from South Africa to Japan. Furthermore, it's one of the few games that is widely inclusive. While you can play with as few as eight people, the most fun is to have a whole class doing battle on the field *Braveheart*-style. It's a game that has left its mark on history as well as on the arms and abdomens of many past players.

WHAT'S THE POINT?

The idea is simple: your team must capture all the opposing players and bring them onto your side. If there is a time limit to the game—in other words, the school bell—the team with the most players at the end of that time wins. What is unique is that while there are singular captains of each team, and all of the action is based on calling out individuals, the victory is very much shared by all members of the team.

HOW YOU PLAY

1 Pick your crew

Two captains are chosen and designate who gets Firsts. Once that's done, they take turns choosing people to build their teams. After the selection process, there will be two teams with the same number of people.

Coach Says . . .

When lining up her team, a captain should make sure that there are as few weak links as possible. One way is to alternate strong and weak players so there are no easy breakage points.

2 Take your sides

The two teams stand facing each other in two parallel lines about 15 feet apart, with teammates joining hands. It is tradition that the captains take the center position on their respective teams.

3 The decision

The captain's team who picked second gets to make the first call. This is the decision to "invite" one of the other team's players to "come over." But, it's not for tea and biscuits. The decision can be solely the captain's or there can be a huddle where the team—hands still joined—curls around to consult with the captain.

4 The call

Once the player on the other team has been chosen, the team makes the call—a public proclamation of challenge. While there are many slight variations, the most common call is:

Red Rover, Red Rover,
Let [player's name] come over!

The called-out person now must run across the No Man's Land toward the other team. They can choose any gap between two players to attempt to run through.

5 The moment of contact
When the runner makes contact there are two outcomes:

- They break through: if they run through the clasped hands of the team, they are able to return to their original team—plus, they are able to bring over one of the opposing players that they broke through along with them. In other words, the team that called them is now one player down.

- They don't break through: if they aren't able to run through the clasped hands of the other team, they must now join that team. They enter the line at the place where they were stopped and now join hands with the players who just minutes ago were their opponents.

6 The favor returned
This process now repeats for the length of the game—alternating teams. They decide who to call over, make the announcement, and try to stop them from breaking the chain.

7 The winner
If there is no time limit, game play continues until there is only one person left on one team. If that person is stopped from breaking through the opposing team, then the game is over. If they break through, they bring over another player and the play continues. If there is a time limit, the team with the most players wins.

OPTIONAL RULES
One Bring Backs
Players can bring back anyone from the opposing team; they don't have to select one of the people in the link they broke through. This is definitely a high-stakes way to play, but the result is wild changes in the team's strength as the strongest players move back and forth regularly.

SAFETY PATROL:
Red Rover without the Black and Blue

This game can cause serious injuries if you're not careful. Both the runners and the line members can get hurt. In most cases, it will be bumps and bruises. But the injuries could be more serious. To reduce injury but keep Red Rover alive, we recommend keeping to the following 5-point plan:

1 Pick a soft, clear area

It is best to play on soft grass in a flat, level field. Since momentum will carry players well beyond the line, make sure there are no hills, trees, or streets close by.

2 Clasp hands not wrists

One of the simplest but most important rules is to insist that players hold hands—palm to palm. While this is easier to break through, it prevents serious injuries from runners hitting an unbreakable human wall.

3 Below the shoulder line

The team trying to make the stop must keep their hands below the shoulder level of the runner. This prevents the possibilities of clotheslining the neck or striking the face.

4 Shorter running starts

Some people play with the teams standing over 30 feet apart. While this looks impressive, it allows for the runners to build up too much speed—and potentially cause too much injury.

5 No fist-forward formations

Not only is it a tongue twister, it's dangerous. A fist-forward formation is when players hold out their interlocked hands in a fist between each other, so when the runner comes toward them, he gets a sock in the gut. This is both unsportsmanlike and unsafe.

WORLD OF PLAY

A traditional Japanese game called Hana Ichi Monme is similar to Red Rover but with a longer rhyming song and instead of breaking the chain, two players do Rock-Paper-Scissors to determine who is captured.

Breakthrough Pair Bring Backs

Players can bring over both of the opposing players that they broke through. This causes a large swing in player count on each side. This would only be recommended with extremely large teams. Or extremely short time windows.

EXPERT STRATEGIES

While it might not seem like it, Red Rover is more than just running across a field to smash into your friends. There are several strategies and techniques that you can use to take your game to the next level.

Sending Side Techniques

[1] **THE FLING:** This technique involves the whole line of the runner's team pulling back and flinging the runner forward in a whip motion to give her more momentum to break through the opposing line.

[2] **THE SNEAK ATTACK:** Since the runner can choose where to break through the line, expert players use some misdirection to catch opponents off guard by making a hard cut in one direction.

[3] **THE SIDE DRIVE:** Runners can increase their chances of breaking through with the help of physics. By turning slightly to one side, their force gets focused and pushes harder against waiting hands.

[4] **THE BATTLE CRY:** Runners can also increase their chances with the help of psychology. Scream a battle cry just before you break through to frighten your opponents into shying away from you as you run at them.

Receiving Side Techniques

[1] **THE SAPLING STRATEGY:** There is an African proverb that says: "The wind does not break a tree that bends." Likewise, an expert receiving technique is to try to cushion the impact by allowing the line to give a little—instead of holding firm.

[2] **THE REVERSE BATTLE CRY:** While it can't be done every time, when the game is on the line, a coordinated scream from the line is enough to slow down or confuse the runner a bit. And every bit matters in Red Rover.

More Pushing Games

Red Rover is just one of several roughhousing games that involve gratuitous physical contact, but still stop short of full-scale tackling.

BULL IN THE RING

This is a hybrid of Red Rover and tag. One player stands in the middle of a circle of players—all holding hands according to the Red Rover safety method. The player in the center is the bull and is trying to escape the ring by breaking through the hands. When she does, the players who made the circle now pursue the bull on the "loose." The first one to "catch" the bull by tagging her now becomes the next bull.

KING OF THE HILL

This group game requires a soft grassy or even snowy area with a slight mound. The hill in question is more ceremonial than anything. What's not just ceremonial is the age-old quest to capture and defend one's domain. The player who wins Firsts becomes the king and ascends the hill. Simply stated, he must protect it from the other players looking to dethrone him—by knocking him off the hill. As with all power struggles, the next king is determined not by who knocked off the king, but who scrambles to the top of the hill first after the void is created. Score one for the opportunists!

SHOVE WINTER OUT

If King of the Hill symbolizes timeless human power struggles, this game symbolizes the struggle with Mother Nature. At least six players are needed to divide into Team Winter and Team Summer. A 15-foot circle is marked in the ground or snow. Winter starts inside the circle and Summer outside. All the players keep their arms crossed across their chests. At "go!" the Team Summer enters the circle and attempts to push and shove Team Winter out of the circle. Once out, the Winter players switch sides and join the Summer force. Once all Winter players are out, they reverse roles, and start again.

BULLDOG

The original game from Britain is also called Octopus, Bullrush, Pom-Pom Pullaway, and Running Bases. One player (or two) is the bulldog and stands in middle of a small field. The rest of the players stand in a line at on one side. The goal is to cross the field without being "bitten" (tagged) by one of the bulldogs. If a player is caught, he joins the bulldogs for the next round. The winner is the last remaining player to cross without getting tagged.

LEG WRESTLING
Good, Clean, Getting Dirty Fun

WHAT IT IS

There are types of wrestling, like Thumb Wrestling, that have reduced the full-body effort of traditional wrestling into one limited area to create a safer, more universal appeal. Leg Wrestling is the opposite. It involves a lot of contact, a lot of time on the ground, and two players who aren't afraid to get close and get dirty to have some good clean fun.

WHAT'S THE POINT?

Unlike every other form of wrestling, the goal here is, in essence, to *unpin* your opponent. Each player starts where other forms of wrestling end—with their backs on the ground. The winner is the one that pries the other off the ground with the sheer force of one's legs.

HOW YOU PLAY

1 Well-matched matchup

This game is best played between people of evenly matched size and strength. And, since there is a lot of physical contact, players should be of the same gender.

2 Take it laying down

Before getting on the ground, take time to survey the area for any objects that might hurt you or other players. Once the designated area is clear, two players lie flat on their backs, side-by-side, pointing in different directions so the feet of one player are next to the head of the other, and the players' hips are touching.

③ The count up

Players hook their right arms at the elbow, and then count out loud as they raise and lower their right legs three times. When they get to the number three, they lock their legs behind their knees (see illustration) and commence the leg wrestling.

④ The struggle

Without using any other body parts other than their right arms and legs, players attempt to force their opponent to raise their back off the floor. Players must remain locked the whole time and can only use their left arms and legs for balance.

SAFETY PATROL: Unlike pro wrestling, leg wrestling is very real and injuries can happen if players aren't careful. Be sure to make a rule that if either one of the players says ouch, or any other phrases denoting pain, both players must stop immediately.

Coach Says . . .

More than any other wrestling game, Leg Wrestling is about speed right at the start to gain an immediate advantage— and a trip to Winnersville.

More Wrestling Games

Wrestling is possibly the most primal form of play—for humans and animals alike. It's pure competition with just enough structure to prevent real harm, but enough actual physical contact to break a sweat without breaking anything else.

ARM WRESTLING

This legendary strong-arm test is a great recess game too. It requires a table so that two opponents can face each other head on. The elbows on their wrestling arms must maintain contact with the table to prevent body weight from being used as leverage. The players clasp hands and, at the signal, attempt to force the back of their opponent's hand down toward the table. The first to force their opponent's knuckles to the tabletop, wins.

STANDING HAND WRESTLING

Don't let the name fool you, this contest involves the whole body. Two players face each other with their right feet touching—left feet are about a shoulder's lengths back. Players clasp right hands to begin the match and try to make each other lose balance. They cannot use their left hands (which must remain on their hips) or make any contact with the other player other than the grip.

ONE-LEGGED HAND WRESTLING

In this variation of the game, opponents start facing each other and use their left hands to hold their left legs off the ground. In a similar manner to Hand Wrestling, the players clasp right hands and attempt to knock the other off balance. The first player to let go of their left foot or touch the ground loses. This game will produce a lot of erratic pogoing, making the spectators the real winners.

BUTT BOXING

This game is great for group battle—a combination of sumo wrestling and twerking. All of the players bend at the knees and lock their forearms together behind their knees under their buttocks. They then waddle, hop, or bounce backward to try to knock into the other players. When a player is knocked over or releases their arms, they are out. The last player squatting wins!

WORLD OF PLAY

In Brazil, there is a game called Luta de Galo, Portuguese for "fight of the roosters." It is played by two players who each have a handkerchief hanging out of a pocket. Each player hops on one foot and uses only one arm to try to steal their opponent's handkerchief.

TAG GAMES
Chasing, Fleeing . . . Tag, You're It!

Game Stats

STYLE: Pursuit and capture
PLAYERS: Four or more
REQUIREMENTS:
Open space
SKILLS:
Stamina
Agility
Speed
Evading

WHAT IT IS

Tag is not just one of the most exciting games on the playground, it's one of the most significant. It taps into our hunter instincts to follow and stalk prey. It sets off our fight-or-flight response—making us run for our metaphoric lives. Ultimately, it speaks to our desire to avoid being excluded from the tribe—or in the words of the game, we don't want to be It. But thinking about all of this heavy stuff can ruin the fact that Tag is just as fun as all get out.

WHAT'S THE POINT?

The whole point of tag is for the person who is It to make someone else It instead of them. Yep, it's just that simple, which is why it's so dang fun!

HOW YOU PLAY

1 Tag, You're It!

Start by deciding Firsts to designate who will be It. That player chases all the other players, trying to touch or "tag" one of them. If she succeeds, the person she tagged is now It and tries to chase everyone else. The game continues until everyone is exhausted or it's time to go home. The real fun comes in the multitude of game play variations.

ADDITIONAL RULES

Home Base and Jail

Before playing, all players should agree on a designated area to be used as a home base or jail. This can be a structure or area where a player can run to for safety and protection from whoever is It. Players are only allowed to use home base when being chased, and can only stay on home base for a short time—typically around 10 seconds. In some variations, home base is turned into a jail where tagged players can wait while the game continues.

WORLD OF PLAY

In Australia, Tag is also called Tiggy.

TAGGING TECHNIQUES

The rules may be easy, but properly tagging a player is harder than you think.

Good Tagging

- Tag using an open hand or fingers
- Lightly touch on the back, shoulders, or body
- Make verbal confirmation like "gotcha," "tag," or "you're It!"

Bad Tagging

- Closed fist tagging
- Hard contact or pushing that might cause a player to fall
- Grabbing clothes or hair
- Tags to the head or face

Standing Tag

As a player tries to fake you out and run past you, crouch down low with your arms bent and ready at your sides. Use your legs to pivot toward the proper direction as you extend your arms to tag your victim.

Running Tag

When chasing down a fleeing player, timing is critical. Don't just run after the player with your arms outstretched. Chase him down running with regular form, pumping your arms to gain speed, and extend your arms at the very last second when you're within reach.

Flying Leap Tag

Once you've mastered the standing and running techniques, adding this split second adjustment will help you gain some extra distance. If your opponent is still beyond reach and you are on a soft surface, jump or dive directly toward their torso as you extend your arm in a Superman pose. Make contact, wow the crowd, and proudly yell out "tag!"

Coach Says . . .

No matter what technique you're using, always keep your eye on your opponent's hips. Do not focus on the head or shoulders since they can more easily fake you out.

WORLD OF PLAY

In Israel, there is a variation of Duck Duck Goose called Black Rabbit. Instead of calling "duck," the It player says a color and then "rabbit" (for example, "Green rabbit") as they tap players on the head. When they're ready to pick someone, they call out, "Black rabbit" instead of "goose."

EVADING TECHNIQUES

1 **Juke (a.k.a. Stutter Step, Shake & Back):** While running, shift your feet and focus in one direction, only to fake out your pursuer at the last moment by going in another direction.

2 **Plant and Go:** Run at an angle and plant a foot as if going one direction, (getting them to commit) and then quickly switch directions.

3 **Side Twist:** Turn your torso 90 degrees while still running to move just out of reach of the It player's outstretched arms.

4 **Spin Move:** A complete spin that should be performed in midstride. This technique is simple, effective, and dizzying.

5 **Corner Cut:** If you are being chased from behind and have the benefit of large obstacles nearby, try to break the It player's line of sight on you by making a sharp, unexpected move behind an object as soon as you're out of view.

OTHER WAYS TO PLAY: BASIC TAGGING GAMES

Here is a full rundown of classic and wildly popular Tag games. Try them, improve on them, make them your own.

Blob Tag (a.k.a. Build Up, Amoeba Tag)

In Blob Tag, when a player gets tagged, they must join hands with the It player and form a blob or chain. Anyone in the blob can tag a free player, so the blob continues to get bigger and bigger as the game goes on. The game ends when all players are "eaten" by the blob.

Duck Duck Goose

Duck Duck Goose starts with a group of typically five or more players, sitting cross-legged in a circle facing toward the center. The It player (a.k.a. the "fox") walks around the circle clockwise, tapping each player and calling them a "duck" until he decides to designate a player of his choice as a "goose." Then, the goose must jump up and chase the fox around the circle. If the fox makes it all the way around and sits in the goose's free spot, the goose becomes the fox. If the goose tags the fox before he reaches the open spot, the fox remains It.

Freeze Tag (a.k.a. Stuck-in-the-Mud)

The player who is It remains so the entire game and chases the other players. When a free player is tagged, they must instantly stop and freeze in place. That player can be unfrozen if they are tagged by a free player. The game ends when everyone is frozen. The last person frozen is It for the next round.

Man from Mars

The It player—the man from Mars—starts the game by standing in the middle of the playing area while the other players (earthlings) stand in a line at one end of the area facing the man from Mars. The earthlings begin by chanting out "Man

FUN FACT

One variation of Freeze Tag is Tunnel Tag—a player can only be unfrozen if another free player crawls through the frozen player's legs. In another, TV Tag, to unfreeze someone a free player must tag a frozen player while also yelling out the name of a TV show.

Coach Says . . .

The weirder the spot, the funnier it is to watch your opponents try to run, so make sure your tag lands on a strategic body part.

from Mars, man from Mars, will you take us to the stars?" The man from Mars then replies with "Only if you're wearing . . ." and yells out a color. Any earthlings wearing that color are safe and can walk to the opposite side while the other players must run to the other side and try avoid getting tagged. Tagged players become It and join the man from Mars in the next round. Play continues until only one earthling remains.

Poison Tag

All players must keep both hands on their chest at all times during the game. The It player can tag with one free hand but must always keep his other hand on his chest while chasing. Play like regular tag, but when someone gets tagged, they become It and team up with the It player to tag everyone else. However the tagged player(s) must always keep one hand on the exact spot the got tagged for the rest of the game, no matter where it is. This is the poison spot and it can get really fun(ny) when you tag someone in a hard to reach spot. The last person who survives by not getting poisoned wins and is It first for the next round.

Zombie Tag

The It player is the first infected zombie. When the zombie tags another player, that player also becomes a zombie. Zombies are not allowed to run, just walk fast with both arms outstretched at all times. No one can defeat the zombies, so the game continues until everyone is infected, except the last player left uninfected—who is the winner!

SAFETY PATROL: Make sure you play Blind Man's Bluff in an open area free of dangerous items that can cause injury if the It player hits, trips, or slips on something.

OTHER WAYS TO PLAY: HIDING GAMES

In these Tag games, players hide from each other to add a whole new level of surprise and mischief.

Blind Man's Bluff

The It player is blindfolded and counts to ten while the other players scatter and hide in plain sight. Once the It player yells out "ten!" all players must freeze wherever they are and the It player gropes around trying to find them. Players are allowed to make noises to try and trick the It player into changing directions. Once the It player finally tags someone, that player become It and the game starts over.

Hide and Seek

The It player covers her eyes and counts out loud up to thirty while the other players go off and hide. Once the It player is done counting she shouts, "Ready or not, here I come!" and seeks out the hidden players. When she finds and tags a player, that player must wait at home base until the game is over. The game ends when the It player finds all the other players. The last player found is the winner and become It for the next round. However, if the It player can't find all the players after a long time, the caught players at home base can force the It player to call out "Olly olly oxen free!" and the game starts over with all the hidden players returning to home base.

Kick the Can

An empty soda can, or something similar, is placed in the playing area. The It player covers his eyes and counts while all the other players hide. When the It player finds and tags another player, that player must go to jail—a designated spot decided before the game begins. At any time, a free player can kick the can and set all the jailed players free. Play continues until all the free players are caught.

Sardines

This is like Hide and Seek in reverse. (And no, that's not Seek and Hide.) One player is the "sardine" and goes out and finds a hiding spot where she can lay down. The remaining players break apart and hunt for the hider. When someone finds her, they ask, "Are you the sardine?" The hider answers, "Yes I am." At this point the player must join the

FUN FACT

There are many spins on "Olly Olly Oxen Free!" such as "Ollie Ollie Umphrey," "Olly-Olly-ee," "Outtie Outtie Lets be Free," and "Ollie Ollie in Come Free."

sardine, lying next to her. This continues until each subsequent hunter joins the growing group of sardines. The last player to find the location loses the game and becomes the sardine for the next round.

OTHER WAYS TO PLAY: TEAM GAMES

In these tag variations all players are split into two even groups to battle it out as a team.

Cops and Robbers (a.k.a. Jail, Prisoner)

Players are split into two even teams: cops and robbers. The cops are It and must chase down and tag the robbers. As each robber gets tagged, they must go to a designated jail or area and remain there until free robbers jailbreak them by tagging. The game is over when all the robbers are in jail. The roles are then reversed in the next round.

Crows and Cranes

Players start by splitting into two even teams—the crows and the cranes—and then setting up the playing field with two end lines and two lines a short distance apart in the center of the field.

Teams set up in a line standing side by side on the center lines with each team facing each other. To begin, a neutral player—the bird caller—is positioned between both teams and calls out either "crows" or "cranes." The called team must immediately turn around and run toward their end line. The other team then chases them and tries to tag players before they cross the end line. Any players tagged become a member of the opposite team. Each team then lines up again to begin the next round. This continues until there's only one player left on one of the teams. That player is the winner and becomes the bird caller for the next round.

Coach Says . . .

To make Crows and Cranes more exciting, the bird caller can vary the calls by holding and extending out the "crrrr" sound, or trick the players by calling out other words with the crrrr sounds, like crack, crust, cry baby, etc.

WORLD OF PLAY

The most important word in the world might just be "It." Here is a sampling of Tag games from around the world.

KABADDI

Originating in India over 4,000 years ago, this game requires two teams and a field divided in half with a rope or a line drawn in chalk. Teams line up about 20 feet from back on either side of the line. One team sends a player across the line to tag out as many of the opposing players as possible. The rub is that he can only stay on that side while chanting "*kabaddi-kabaddi-kabaddi-kabaddi-kabaddi-kabaddi*" without taking a breath. The other team can try to prevent him from returning—so if he breathes or stops chanting he is considered out. The sides alternate offense and defense with each session.

CATCH THE DRAGON'S TAIL

This traditional Chinese game starts with a line of at least ten players—standing with both hands on the person in front of them. The first person is the head of the dragon, and they must catch the last person, the tail. If they do, the tail player becomes the new head and the wiggly fun continues.

BIMBO

There's more to this classic Italian schoolyard game than just a silly name. The player who is It is the Bimbo and stands between two lines of players about 15 to 20 feet apart with their hands cupped behind their backs. The Bimbo holds two small leaves and walks behind the lines—sneakily placing the leaves in two of the players' hands. Then the Bimbo returns to the center of the two lines and calls, "Stop! thief! lucky leaf!" At that point the two players with the leaves must cross to the other side before the Bimbo catches them. They give the leaf to another player, like in the game Hot Potato. The first player who gets tagged while holding the leaf becomes the next Bimbo.

Steal the Bacon

Players divide themselves into two teams while a neutral player gets picked as the referee. Players then decide a call sign (a number between one and ten), and then share that number with a member of the other team and the referee. Each team lines up on opposite sides of the playing area, placing the "bacon" (any small object, like a ball or a flag) in the center. The game starts when the referee announces a call sign. The team members who know that call sign must run to the center, grab the bacon, and return back to their side without being tagged by anyone on the opposing team. When a player successfully brings home the bacon, that team wins! To make things interesting, the referee is allowed to call more than one call sign, which makes for many pairs of players, each player attempting to steal the bacon.

ADVANCED VARIATIONS

These sportier versions of Tag add more skill, challenge, and sometimes extra equipment to the mix.

Capture the Flag

Start by splitting up into two teams of three or more people and create bases for each team by splitting up the play area (streets, trails, creeks, and fence lines all make good borders). Designate a couple of items as flags (old T-shirts or even large sticks can work) and display each team's flag in an area on their base. Each team then attempts to grab the other team's flag through any means necessary all while doing their best to defend their own flag.

Once a player has the other team's flag, he must make a run for his own base. If any of the other team's players tag him before he makes it, that player is then captured and placed in the other team's jail and the flag is put back in its post. Players can free jailed teammates by tagging them. If they are tagged by the other team in the process, however, then they get stuck in jail as well. This continues until a team either captures the flag or until an entire team is stuck in jail.

Flashlight Tag (a.k.a. Spotlight)

Flashlight Tag is played in the dark and instead of tagging another player with your hand, the It player holds a flashlight and tags a free player by shining the light on them, "hitting" them with the light beam. Once hit by the light, that player is out and must wait at home base. The game is over when all free players have been tagged by the light—the last player hit is It for the next round.

Spud

All players start standing in a circle with the It player in the middle holding a rubber playground ball and starting the game by throwing the ball high up into the air. As soon as the ball is thrown, all the other players run off but must immediately freeze as soon as It catches the ball and shouts "SPUD!" The It player then takes three big steps and throws the ball, trying to hit any frozen player of their choice. If a frozen player gets hit, they become It and the game starts over from the beginning. If It misses, the game continues with all the players unfrozen in their current position and It throws the ball up again starting another round.

Coach Says . . .

Army Tag is a fun "one-up" version of Flash Light Tag in which a player who is out can get rescued from home base by another free player—similar to Cops and Robbers.

King Chase Queen

This one-on-one version of Tag is a boy vs. girl battle royale that involves a "King" (the boy), and a "Queen" (the girl). To start, the King and Queen each must balance an object called the "crown" (traditionally a classic chalkboard eraser) on their head. A third player called the "Judge" must cover her eyes and order the players by shouting "King chase Queen" or "Queen chase King," and the King and Queen must follow the orders trying to tag or escape one another. At any time, the Judge can yell out the opposite order and the players must switch roles immediately. If the King tags the Queen, he gets a point and visa-versa. If either player's crown falls off at any time during the game the other player gets a point. First player to reach 5 points wins.

Coach Says . . .

King Chase Queen is a great game to try indoors where there's a lot of furniture to meander between. If you can't find an eraser to balance use a small book, a deck of playing cards, a candy bar, or some other small, flat, and safe object.

Muckle (a.k.a. Catch the Carrier, Rumble Fumble)

This extreme Tag game is actually the complete opposite of traditional tag. In Muckle, all the other players chase the lone It player! Here's how to play:

NO SCORE VERSION

The It player starts with a ball, usually a football but almost any ball will do.

The rest of the players chase the It player trying to tag him with two hands. Once properly tagged, the It player must then toss the ball straight up in the air and the other players gather around until someone decides to pick it up and run away. The game continues until no one has any energy left.

SCORING VERSION

Play in a defined area with two end lines and sidelines. Tennis or basketball courts both make great choices.

Start at one end line and the It player tries to cross the end line with the ball in an attempt to make it across the field to the opposite end line. If he can make it all the way and cross the opposite end line, that player scores 1 point and starts again toward the opposite end line.

If a player two-hand tags the It player, he must drop the ball at the spot of the tag. Any other player can pick the ball up and continue to the end line.

Coach Says . . .

A two-hand tag is not as easy as it sounds. Both hands must touch the player at the same time. If each hand touches but not at the same time this is called a "pitty pat." Pitty pats don't count as a clean tag.

Victory Celebrations

When all the taunting is said and the games are done: Winning is not the most important thing. But, for the record, it is a great thing and there is no better way to conclude recess than with a victory celebrations.

THE CLASSIC HIGH FIVE

Nothing celebrates a well-earned win like two hands meeting in midair to make that perfect popping clap. The high five has always been and always will be one of the best ways to celebrate a victory. Not only does it look cool, but it's versatile, too! This classic move can be done high, low, solo, or with a big group and it always looks good.

THE FIST BUMP

Each player makes a fist and, with a soft push, bumps fists in midair at the knuckles. This one is great for a quick, quiet celebration, and it's even less likely to transmit germs during cold season.

THE FLYING BACK-TO-BACK

Made famous by professional athletes, this midair maneuver involves running towards your teammate, leaping into the air, and then turning your backs so they collide in an elegant flying, twisting showcase of strength and dominance. Alternate versions include the side shoulder bump and the jumping butt bump.

THE CARRY OFF

Getting carried off by a group of adoring fans and teammates is something everyone dreams about and is the very reason why some people play in the first place. Show your star player just how great he is by picking him up together and carrying him off into the sunset.

ACKNOWLEDGMENTS

The authors would like to thank all the players out there: the kids and kids at heart, the teachers and gym teachers, the cool parents and understanding neighbors, everyone who helped bring the fun times into our lives. We'd also like to thank Stephanie Kip Rostan and Monika Verma at Levine Greenberg Rostan; Courtney Drew, Emily Haynes, and the rest of the team at Chronicle Books; and MacFadden & Thorpe for bringing this fun book to life.

CONTRIBUTORS

A big high five goes out to all the help from our recess experts Julia Askin, Nick Benas, Ben Blatt, Sean Effel with Squarefour.com, Steve Frasher, Julian Gluck with FingerJoust.com, Mike Judd, Sam Kass at SamKass.com, Duncan Little, David Lowry with Kickball.com, Ed Prentiss with theNDL.com, Alex Smith, and Chris Spatola.

REFERENCE

1. Jarret, O.S. "Recess in elementary school: What does the research say?" (2002). Accessed January 18, 2015 http://www.ericdigests.org/2003-2/recess.html

2. Boone, J.L., and J.P. Anthony. "Evaluating the impact of stress on systemic disease: the MOST protocol in primary care." *Journal of American Osteopathic Association* (2003).

3. "The Benefits of Play for Adults," HelpGuide.org, accessed January 18, 2015, http://www.helpguide.org/life/creative_play_fun_games.htm

4. Poundstone, William. *Rock Breaks Scissors: A Practical Guide to Outguessing and Outwitting Almost Everybody*. Little, Brown and Company, 2014.

5. Wang, Zhijian, and Bin Xu, "Social Cycling and Conditional Responses in the Rock-Paper-Scissors Game." *Scientific Reports*. (2014) doi: 10.1038/srep05830

ABOUT THE AUTHORS

Ben Applebaum is the author of over half a dozen humor books. He is also creative director, speaker, and retired (self-proclaimed) Hand Slap champion. He and his wife have two daughters, Gillian and Miranda, who have helped him step up his Clapping Game skills.

Dan DiSorbo is principal of PB&J Design, an award-winning brand design consultancy; and coauthor and illustrator of several pop-culture and humor books. In his spare time he is an avid gamesman and loves playing serious matches of Rock-Paper-Scissors and Hide and Seek with his wife and two sons in Connecticut. More info at PBJDesign.com.

Michael Ferrari is a freelance writer and a creative marketing specialist. He's also a vicious Dodgeball player and an unrivaled Thumb Wrestling champion. He lives with his wife, son, and dog in the Philadelphia suburbs. More info at MichaelFerrariCreative.com.